THE POWER INDEX METHOD

THE POWER INDEX METHOD

For Profitable Futures Trading

By
HAROLD GOLDBERG

Windsor Books, Brightwaters, New York

Published by Windsor Books
P. O. Box 280
Brightwaters, N.Y., 11718

Manufactured in the United States of America

ISBN 0-930233-73-5

Harold Goldberg

Mr. Harold Goldberg has had extensive experience covering three decades as a researcher, writer, advisor and account executive. He is also the author of *Advanced Commodity Spread Trading,* published in 1985. His two books are the culmination of 30 years of trial and error toward finding the key to futures market movements.

Acknowledgement

My sincere thanks to Debra Rofheart who so painstakingly edited and typed this manuscript. Her superb editing and typing have produced a masterful manuscript.

TABLE OF CONTENTS

Introduction

I want to talk to you about me; my style, my opinions and what my book can do for you. No, I am not being conceited— far from it. This is an introduction, and it is my belief that the author should develop a personal bridge between himself and the reader of his book. The following pages will help you become acquainted with me and my thinking as regards to profitable trading.

The language, at times, is somewhat colorful. Particularly when I talk about some of the people in this business who, in my opinion, seduce the unsuspecting public. They are the ladies or gentlemen of the evening (depending on one's proclivities in that area of desire). I am referring to Account Executives (AE's), many of whom have been given the title of Vice President. In a chapter near the end of the book, I will tell you how to protect yourself from AE's. They can be a most unscrupulous lot.

Be advised, here and now, that positively, absolutely, and unequivocally a fast reading of the methodology I will teach you will *not* make you rich.

However, I can and I will categorically state that trading futures contracts affords you the possibility to make money. And the techniques presented in this book will aid you in that quest. How much you will make, I don't know. Some readers will generate more profits than others. It will depend on the amount of capital you employ, how well you learn the methodology presented and, certainly, on your emotional make-up.

In essence, we will be working as a team—a one-to-one teacher/student situation. In time, you will know my thinking simply by the words I use to describe a situation. But have no fear, I will make my reasoning quite clear at all times.

In the English language, there is a word to describe many parts of this book. The word is "redundant." According to *The American Heritage Dictionary,* one of a number of definitions for the word redundant is, "exceeding what is necessary or natural." It is my opinion that a teacher should include as many ways of looking at something as possible. Not everyone sees or understands a subject in the same way or from the same point of view. So, redundant I will be, in the belief that there is nothing redundant about making money! Bear with me and by the time you have finished this book, you will know what to do, when to do it and why it should be done a certain way when it comes to making your trading decisions.

Chapter 1

Important Preliminaries

What you learn in this book can be put to use immediately. You will not be subjected to any "hocus-pocus" by word or deed.

You will be pleasantly surprised to know that there are no algebraic equations any place in this book. Most people I have met cannot work with that type of math, so out it goes, with no loss at all to you. If you can do simple arithmetic, composed of addition, subtraction, multiplication and division, I will make an effective futures trader out of you. The simple arithmetic, and I stress the word *simple*, can be done by hand or with a $5.00 calculator. The only difference is that the calculator is faster.

A caveat: As you study, try not to let your mind wander. If you have experience with bar charts, P&F charts, moving averages, oscillators, technical formations, etc., don't think about them. They do not have anything to do with this study. We do use graphs, but they do not incorporate the afore-mentioned factors.

It is further suggested that you refrain from "fine tuning" the techniques herein. Certainly they are not the absolute, ultimate and only way as they stand, I'm not that vain. But they do work. *Learn first, experiment later.* In other words, get the theory, the basics, the procedures down pat. Then, if you so choose, improvise. But do yourself a favor, DO IT ON PAPER FIRST!

What you will be studying is a methodology which can be applied to any futures contract listed on any exchange, and any futures contract which is not presently listed.

You see, the methodology or theory is based on measuring the emotions of traders. It does not matter if they are trading T-bonds, sugar, grains, or whatever. Their emotions, which are reflected in their buying and selling decisions (and the strength or conviction of same, by their amout of trading), will tell you what is about to happen to the futures price. That is your edge when you take a position in the futures contract.

The daily price gyrations can play havoc with the emotions of traders. Value, price and worth, therefore, should be understood and placed in proper perspective.

Value is our perception of what something is worth. Price is the amount we are willing to pay for worth. What do worth and price have to do with attempting to project a price trend?

Worth is subjective. That is, we judge worth by the degree of need. How much do we need the wheat? The cumulative effects of the judgement of worth are reflected in the price we are ready to pay for that wheat. Hence, the price is but a reflection of the worth of a product. No more, no less.

If worth, to some extent, is subjective, we have the first part of the theory behind the trading methodology. From the subjectivity of how one values worth, we add actual or perceived needs for the product. We then marry the elements, which, in turn, become demand. How much do we think will be needed and how much will we actually require? The end result is not an absolute, due to events over which we have no control, such as weather, or government interference, etc.

Since nature is oftentimes uncooperative, we cannot be certain that our future needs will be met. This is the core behind price movements which may seem out of line: our subjective and actual needs become ''worthier'' and we are willing to pay a higher price to insure an adequate supply of the commodity at the time it is needed.

Worth is eventually translated into action. Specifically, we will purchase a futures contract to insure delivery at the proper time. Conversely, other users may determine that the worth (to them) is too high and will offer (sell) the futures contract for delivery at some time in the future for a stipulated price.

It is apparent, therefore, that the degree of worth must be measured to profit in the trading of commodity futures. Measuring worth (open interest) and its relationship to value (price) is the concept behind the development of my method. As you work through this book, keep in mind that it is *worth* which determines price and not the other way around. This worth effects the valuation of the futures contract price.

Open interest in a futures contract represents an equal number of longs and shorts. For every long side of a contract, there is a short side. In other words, for each trader who is long a contract, there is a trader who is short the same contract. Each side of the contract is claimed by someone, so to speak. It would seem that, price-wise, we are at an impasse—one long trader who believes the price is going higher and one short trader who believes the price is going lower. A stalemate, or so it would seem.

What is the catalyst that gets the price moving? In one word—*fear*. A buyer (long) of a futures contract goes long because he fears that the price will move higher and he will miss a potential "long" profit. A trader who is short the same contract is short because he fears that he will lose a potential profit if the price goes down without him. What gets the price moving is whose fear is stronger.

The question I asked was: "If the fear quotient of the buyer (long) is stronger than that of the seller (short), what would be the result?" I then proceeded to turn the question around, "If the fear quotient of the seller is higher than that of the buyer, what then would be the result, price-wise?" The next question is, "How do I measure the fear quotient to take advantage of the dichotomy?"

The answer to the first question: If the buyer's fear quotient is higher than that of the seller, the buyer will increase his bid

15

(pay a higher price) for the futures contract. This will drive the price of the contract up. If the seller's fear quotient is higher than that of the buyer, the seller (short side) will accept a lower price, reasoning that the price has further to fall and he, in turn will profit. If this is the prevailing attitude in the market, the price will fall. This answers the second question.

The answer to the third question is a little more involved. For one thing, the fear relationship of the traders on the long and short side of the contract is complicated by the often false signals of the closing price. Using the closing price alone as an indicator of fear will have you running around in circles. A closing price, on any given day, can do one of three things relative to the previous day's closing price: it can close higher, lower or unchanged.

The unreliability of the closing price as a true indicator of fear forces us to look elsewhere. I turned my attention to the often-times wide price fluctuations of intra-day trading, fluctuations which sometimes reached limit proportions up and down. These intra-day swings, as it turned out, *were* the barometer of the degree of fear, relative to anticipated future price action—irrespective of the closing price!

Based on my theory that fear moves contract prices, you will learn how to obtain, graph and use a fear index, applied to individual futures contracts so as to profitably trade any of them.

I will, in fact, call this a Power Index. Based on fear, it shows who (buyers or sellers) has the power in the market. It also is a good indicator of how much power they have. And consequently, how strong each up or down move will be.

Chapter 2

Fear—The Price Motivator

Fear intensity is measurable. It can be quantified. You are going to learn how to quantify the fear quotient of traders. And then you'll learn how it best can be graphed. At that time, you will be able to visually see which way the Power Index is moving and determine the probable direction of the price of the futures contracts.

THE POWER INDEX VALUATION FORM

There are two parts to this form. The top section contains the following information: the name of the futures contract and the trading month of the contract. Underneath are eight columns, each with a heading as follows: Column 1—Date, 2—High, 3—Low, 4—Close, 5—Average Price, 6—% Change, 7—Open Interest, and 8—Adjusted Open Interest.

In an earlier part of this book, I asked you to refrain from thinking about tangential subjects such as bar line charts, etc. I am making that request again. For the time being, forget any questions which may pop into your mind. The step-by-step procedures, as I will outline them, should answer any and all questions.

Now, let's just focus on the Power Index Valuation Form.

Column 1—Date. Each day insert the date. Its purpose is to give you a time-frame reference.

Column 2—High. In this column you insert the highest price the futures contract reached in trading that day.

Column 3—Low. In this column you insert the lowest price the futures contract reached that day.

Column 4—Close. In this column you insert the closing price for the futures contract for that day.

Column 5—Average Price. In this column, insert the total of the high, low, and closing price, divided by 3.

Column 6—Percent (%) Change. You insert in this column the difference between today's average price and yesterday's average price in terms of a percent. The computation for this figure is discussed in the next chapter.

Chapter 7—Open Interest ("OI"). In this column you will insert the OI amount as listed in the newspaper. More on this shortly.

Column 8—Adjusted Open Interest. The Adjusted OI is a cumulative index. It is, in point of fact, a measurement of the ebb and flow of the emotions of traders. Therefore, it is the Power Index. I will use the terms Power Index and Adjusted OI synonymously from this point forward. Briefly, the Adjusted OI is found by multiplying the OI (Col. 7) by the % Change (Col. 6) and adding (or subtracting) that figure to (or from) the Adjusted OI entry of the previous day. This, too, will be thoroughly covered in the next chapter.

Before I conclude this chapter, I want to answer the questions which may have arisen in your mind regarding the gathering of the data. Where you get the data from is the most important question. Most of you will get it from the financial section of your newspaper. The most frequent source consulted, of course, is *The Wall Street Journal.* Your broker can also give you the information and, for those of you with personal computers, there are financial services you can subscribe to which will give you the data, as well.

The rest of this chapter I will devote to a "Question and Answer Period." This will confirm some of the unclear areas I've encountered.

Question: "What do I do if the high, low and closing price are the same?"

Answer: This phenomenon will occur when a contract's price opens limit up or down. Insert the same price in the High, Low, Close and Average Price columns. Then proceed to find the % Change.

Question: "Suppose the Exchange closes early. Do I still use the price and open interest data for that day?"

Answer: Yes. By the way, if the Exchange is closed for a holiday or on the weekend, you do not skip a space on the work form or the graph. Your work is continuous and there should be no breaks on either the form or the graph.

Question: "I'm confused by the closing price. Sometimes it's called the last or settlement price. If there are different prices designating the closing price, what do I do?"

Answer: The last price may be different from the closing price and the settlement price may be different from either the close or the last price. You will use the *settlement* price as the close.

The last price is the price at which a trade took place at the close of trading. To make matters confusing, this is sometimes called the closing price or simply "the close." What may cause this price to change is the result of the Exchange brokers matching up all the buy and sell orders executed at the moment the closing bell sounded.

When all the orders are matched, the settlement price (sometimes called the final price) is known. Depending on the volume of orders executed on the close of trading, fifteen to forty-five minutes may elapse before this price is known.

Newspapers, due to their tight schedules, cannot wait for the settlement price to be available before they go to press. So they will print the last price under the heading "Close." However, corrections are made in the evening edition. While the heading

19

will say close, the price will be the settlement price. If you have a computer data retrieval service, within two hours after the close of trading, you will have the settlement price.

Question: "If the open interest is missing from the paper, how can I obtain that data?"

Answer: When you see an omission of open interest, don't run out and buy a different newspaper. Chances are, if the open interest is omitted from one paper, none of the others will have the data either. The services which transmit the table of prices, OI, etc., have not included the OI. You are going to have to approximate the data. You can do this on the next trading day. Add the OI of this new trading day to the OI amount of the day before the omission and divide the result by two (2). Use this amount for the missing day's OI. Of course you will have two day's work to do, but that can't be helped. This problem will occur from time to time.

Question: "Suppose the OI has changed dramatically up or down from yesterday's OI, is there something wrong? If so, what can I do?"

Answer: Misprints do happen, not only in the OI figures but in the price data as well. If you see an OI amount, or any other piece of data that is much higher or lower than the level of the last few days, wait until the next trading day. if this new data is back in line with the last five trading days, the figure in question could be an error. Approximate for the erroneous figure in the same manner as outlined for an omission of data, explained above. If the new data is in line with the data you are questioning, assume the data in question to be correct.

Question: "Since today's paper prints OI figures which apply to yesterday's trading, wouldn't using these numbers for today's price action invalidate my work?"

Answer: No. The difference is so negligible, when viewed as a percent, that resulting signals will be valid.

On the next page is the form (Figure 1) that you will be working with. It shows only the name, month and year of the contract, plus the eight columns with their headings.

FIGURE 1
JULY 1984 SUGAR

DATE	HIGH	LOW	CLOSE	AVG.PR.	% CHGE.	OPEN INT.	ADJ. OI

Chapter 3

Finding The Power Index

The procedure is quite easy to master. Believe it or not, the most difficult part of the process is found when working up the average price for T-Bonds, GNMA's or any contract whose value is figured in 32nds. This problem is solved by changing the price to its dollar equivalent. After that, we carry on the computation by adding the three price values (high, low and close) and dividing by 3. If there is a remainder, we round it off to the nearest penny. So don't worry about the arithmetic. All possibilities for obtaining the average price are explored. Rest assured, I will not let you hang.

Step 1. Post the daily data under their respective headings on the form. You will notice, in the sample form (Figure 2) on the next page that the date (4/11/84) is shown twice. The date on the top line is the starting date. Since this is the first day of information, it is again shown under the heading. The date column is not essential. I don't always use it in my own work. I have included it here because it will help you to visualize the time-frame. For instructional purposes, I will use the date column as a reference point to highlight certain data for you as I discuss them in the text. You may choose to either use the date column or simply put in the start date at the top of the sheet. But it is worthwhile to keep as a reference point for your work.

FIGURE 2

JULY 1984 SUGAR

DATE	HIGH	LOW	CLOSE	AVG.PR.	% CHGE.	OPEN INT.	ADJ. OI
4-11-84	6.81	6.65	6.66			26,119	26,119

Notice, too, that the same figure appears in both the OI column and the Adjusted OI column. Again, this is just because it is the first entry, so is not being compared to a prior entry. Therefore, there can be no % Change, and subsequently, no adjustment to the open interest. This blank space in the table will happen every time you start a new contract.

Step 2. Each day post the data from the paper, then figure the Average Price as follows. Add the high, low and close figures and then divide that total by 3. The result is the Average Price, which you will enter under that heading. In the sample form in Figure 3, you will see the Average Price figured for two days, March 26 and 27, 1984, relating to the July 84 Sugar contract. This sample shows what your form will look like with two day's entries.

There are a few things you should notice at this point. First, you will notice the way I abbreviate the date for the second day's entries. While Day 1 shows 3-26-84, Day 2 shows only 27. You can insert the month again when on the first day of a new month. In the interim, it is not necessary to clutter up the column. The same would apply for the year I began to work on a contract. If I started December 31, 1983, the first three date entries on my form would look like this: 12-31-83, 1-4-84, 5 (depending on the first trading day in Jan.). This is really just a time-saver when keeping your records.

Second, look at the average price for sugar on 3-26-84. Were you to do the math, the answer would come out 7.376666666...For our purposes, it is only necessary to be accurate to two places to the right of the decimal point. Therefore, I rounded the average price figure off to 7.38. When the numeral to the right of the decimal is 5 or higher, round up to the next highest whole number, in other words add 1. When the numeral to the right of the decimal is below 5, simply disregard the number. Thus, the calculation for average price on 3-27, was 7.293333...and you will notice that I simply entered 7.29. This rule applies to any average price for all

FIGURE 3
JULY 84 SUGAR

DATE	HIGH	LOW	CLOSE	AVG.PR.	% CHGE.	OPEN INT.	ADJ. OI
3-26-84	7.45	7.24	7.44	7.38	--	22,763	22,763
27	7.45	7.21	7.22	7.29		23,569	

contracts. And simply follows standard elementary mathematical princples.

Third, the OI column contains the OI amount printed in that day's paper. Remember, open interest, as shown in the paper, is the amount for the day before. If the paper heading indicates the price information is for March 26, 1984, the amount of open interest printed therein is for March 25, 1984. However, one day's difference does not affect the work materially, so just use the OI as shown for the days when you are gathering your data. Naturally, if you have access to the correct data that could be used to construct the Power Index.

Step 3. Obtain the Percent Change between each day's average prices. This is how you go about it:

    a. Subtract yesterday's average price from today's average price. Using the data, this would be: 7.29 − 7.38 = −.09. This negative number is the difference between the day's prices.

    b. *Divide* this difference by yesterday's price. You will have the following decimal result: −.09 ÷ 7.38 = .0121951.

    c. To express this figure as a percent, simply multiply it by 100: −.0121951 x 100 = −1.21951, which, rounded to the decimal place we need, is −1.22. This is the figure you enter in the % Change column. You will see it in the sample data in Figure 4.

Please note, if today's average price is lower than yesterday's average price, the % Change will be a negative number, as seen in the sample data. If today's average price is higher than yesterday's average price, the % Change will be a positive number. Just use the minus sign (−) to indicate that the figure is negative. A positive number requires no sign. If there is no difference in price between the two days, simply place a dash (—) in the % Change column.

Also, you *always* find the difference in average price from day to day by *always* subtracting yesterday's price from today's price. Then, you *always* find the percent change by dividing the

27

FIGURE 4
JULY 84 SUGAR

DATE	HIGH	LOW	CLOSE	AVG.PR.	% CHGE.	OPEN INT.	ADJ. OI
3-26-84	7.45	7.24	7.44	7.38	---	22,763	22,763
27	7.45	7.21	7.22	7.29	− 1.22	23,569	22,475

difference by yesterday's average price. *There are no exceptions to these rules.*

Step 4. The last step is to find the amount for the Adjusted Open Interest. This is your Power Index. You compute this figure as follows:

    a. Multiply the open interest (col. 7) by the % Change. Continuing with the sample data, this would produce: -287.54, because $23,569 \times -.01222 = -287.54$.

    b. Remember, 1% is equal to .01 in decimals. That is why we multiply by $-.0122$ instead of -1.22.

    c. The Adjusted OI for today can now be found by subtracting the figure calculated in "a" above from yesterday's Adjusted OI number as follows: $22,763 - 288 = 22,475$. The reason we subtract the 288 (rounded up from 287.54) is because it is a negative number (a negative number always results from a calculation using a negative % Change). If the percent change were positive, the adjusting figure would also be positive and the amount would then be added to yesterday's Adjusted OI to get today's entry. A rule of thumb: negative numbers are subtracted, positive numbers are added.

The procedure employed in obtaining the Adjusted OI (Power Index) is complete. All that remains is the detail of how to convert bond and GNMA prices to their dollar equivalent. When we begin working with these contracts and others, such as the grain complex, I'll teach you how to convert 32nds and fractions into amounts which can be used in our work.

NOTES TO AVOID ERRORS

The average price can never be higher than the highest price reached that day, nor can it be lower than the lowest price reached that day. In other words, if the average price figure you calculate is higher than the entry for the High column, or lower than the entry in the Low column for that day, you have made an error. You have either divided by a number other than 3 or you misadded the numbers. Your average price figure should be a mid-point between the High and Low price for any given day. The only exception is when the contract price has moved locked limit up or down. In that case, the average price will equal the High and Low price, which will be identical.

It is possible for the Adjusted OI to fall below zero. The Adjusted OI moves independently of the open interest. This would occur when the price of the contract has been falling for a long time. Each day you would have a negative % Change, which would give you a negative adjusting figure. After many days of subtracting the adjusting figure from the cumulative number it would eventually be brought below zero. So, it is possible to have a negative Adjusted OI.

Whenever you begin work on a new contract, the first Adjusted OI entry will always be positive. This is because, on the first day of data entry, the Open Interest and Adjusted OI figures are the same number, and Open Interest is always expressed as a positive number. From that point, we add or subtract each subsequent day's adjusting figure and alter the cumulative Adjusted OI figure as appropriate.

The Following Helpful Hints Refer To The Data in Figure 5.

Errors are easy to make. No doubt about it. For example, on 2-3-84, the average price calculated out to be 115.42. Of course it doesn't appear on the work form. The correct number is 165.42, as shown. But I had made a stupid mistake. I point out the error to make a point: Check your work. If a number seems out of line with those prices you have been using, *Recheck*. With prices composed of a decimal, make certain it is in all your calculations, and in the right place. When you add numbers with decimals to whole numbers (no decimals), make

30

FIGURE 5
JUNE 84 S&P 500

DATE	HIGH	LOW	CLOSE	AVG.PR.	% CHGE.	OPEN INT.	ADJ. OI
2- 1-84	168.10	166.85	167.30	167.42	---	1478	1478
2	168.10	166.85	167.85	167.60	+ .0011	1491	1480
3	168.10	163.95	164.20	165.42	- .0130	1524	1460
6	163.80	161.80	161.90	162.50	- .0177	1988	1425
7	163.10	161.15	162.35	162.20	- .0018	2199	1421
8	162.60	158.20	158.50	159.77	- .0150	2280	1387
9	159.75	157.05	158.70	158.50	- .0079	2492	1367
10	159.40	158.40	158.80	158.87	+ .0023	3084	1374
13	158.85	156.20	156.60	157.22	- .0104	3462	1338
14	159.75	157.85	159.60	159.07	+ .0118	3552	1380
15	160.50	158.60	158.80	159.30	+ .0014	3708	1385
16	159.45	158.00	159.25	158.90	- .0025	4196	1375
17	159.75	158.40	158.80	158.98	+ .0005	4479	1377
21	159.20	157.55	157.80	158 18	- .0050	4455	1355
22	158.75	157.15	157.40	157.77	- .0026	4716	1343
23	158.05	155.00	157.85	156.97	- .0051	4783	1319
24	161.55	158.10	161.45	160.37	+ .0217	5767	1444
27	163.55	160.40	161.90	161.95	+ .0099	6136	1505
28	161.60	159.35	159.50	160.15	- .0111	6106	1437
29	161.50	158.90	159.30	159.90	- .0016	7068	1426

sure the decimals are properly aligned. Here's what I mean. Using the data for the June 84 S&P 500 on 2-6-84, I'll show you what can happen if you mess up with your decimal places (wrong) as opposed to when it is done correctly (right).

High	163.80	High	161.90
Low	16180	Low	161.80
Close +	161.90	Close +	161.90
	16505.70		487.50
÷	3	÷	3
Average Price	5501.90 Wrong!	Average Price	162.50 Right!

There will be times when the average price will seem confusing, not only in the S&P 500, but in other contracts as well. The confusion centers around an average price figure which cannot be duplicated in the price movement of the futures contract. For example, the price movement of the S&P 500 is in increments of 5 points. Each point is equal to $5.00. Each incremental move, therefore, is equal to $25.00. A $25.00 move in the S&P 500 price could be, say, from 161.5 to 161.55. The important point here is that the S&P 500 will never show a price of 161.52. In the data for 2-3-84 the average price of 165.42 is a seeming anomaly, because the contract can only register a price ending in a 5 or a 0.

An average price, because it is an average, need not conform to an incremental point move. The average price is used to obtain the % Change and it will appear on the graph to indicate price direction. But the average price will not be used when actually deciding to take any position.

It was stated previously that you didn't really have to include the Date column. You can insert only the starting date for a point of reference. Another time saver is to do away with the % Change column. It is not really necessary to keep a record of the figure, even though you use the number for your calculations. On the next page is a work form outline (Figure 6) without the Date and % Change columns. It would be wise for you to wait until you are comfortable with the routine before omitting these columns in your own work.

And if you're prone to making computational errors, leave them in. The small amount of time you take filling them in can save you major headaches later. But if the calculations are simple to you, any timesaver is welcome.

FIGURE 6

Feb. 1, 1984   JUNE 84 S&P 500

HIGH	LOW	CLOSE	AVG.PR.	OPEN INT.	ADJ. OI

Chapter 4

Preparing Price Data

My original thinking was to explain how you could convert futures prices to dollars and cents as we studied the individual Power Index graphs. But graph interpretation should be devoted to tactics and strategy, not how to convert prices. This chapter, then, is devoted to understanding how to convert futures prices to their dollar equivalents. If you're already familiar with this, feel free to skip ahead to the next chapter.

A.   FINANCIAL FUTURES

The method for converting financial futures prices, which are quoted in 32nds, to their dollar equivalents is really very simple. The two important pieces of information you need to do the conversion are: (1) contracts are traded in 32nds of a percentage point, and (2) a percentage point is equal to $1,000. This information applies to T-Bonds, T-Notes and GNMA contracts.

Armed with that information, we can come to certain conclusions. First, thirty-two thirty-seconds is equal to one percentage point. Secondly, if a 1% move is equal to $1,000, then each 32nd of a percentage point is equal to $31.25. Come to that conclusion by simply dividing: $1{,}000 \div 32 = 31.25$. With these conclusions, you can figure the dollar value of any financial futures contract. Let's try it.

You look in the paper and see that the closing price for a T-Bond contract was 66.10 on a particular day. What is this number telling you? First, the numbers to the left of the decimal point, as with all decimal numbers, indicates a whole number. As has been said, the whole number, or unit of trading for a T-Bond, is a percentage point. This price is telling us that we have 66 whole percentage points. Since we know a percentage point is worth $1,000, we can easily figure out that $66,000 are represented by the numbers to the left of the decimal point ($66 \times 1{,}000 = 66{,}000$). That takes care of the first part.

The numbers to the right of the decimal point indicate, as in all decimal numbers, the fractional part of the whole unit. The only difference is that this isn't 10 units out of 100, but 10 units out of 32. As mentioned previously, T-Bonds trade in 32nds of a percentage point. Thus, the numbers to the right of the decimal, in this example, are trying to tell us there are 10 thirty-seconds represented in the price (10/32). Since we know that a 32nd is worth $31.25, we just multiply that amount by 10 and have the second part of the answer: $10 \times 31.25 = 312.5$. Now, all we have to do is add the two numbers together and we have the total dollar equivalent of a T-Bond contract with a price of 66.10, which is $66,312.50 (66,000 + 312.50).

To make certain you grasp the concept of this price conversion, we will use it to figure the average price for the following data:

	High	**Low**	**Last**
	66.30	65.14	65.20

High	66,000 + 937.50 =	$ 66,937.50
Low	65,000 + 437.50 =	65,437.50
Last	65,000 + 625.00 =	65,625.00
		$198,000.00
	÷	3
		$ 66,000.00 Average Price

B. GRAINS

Whenever I speak about a particular grain contract, the rationale will apply to the other grains, excluding meal and oil. They will be covered separately. Grains trade in dollars, cents, and fractional cents per bushel. A price of wheat, for example, may appear as $3.10¼—three dollars, ten and one-quarter cents.

Grains move in quarter cent increments, i.e., ¼, ½, ¾, and 00. The two zeros indicate the next whole cent above the ¾ price or below the ¼ price. Example: the increment above − 3.10¾ is 3.1100. Conversely, the next lower price beneath 3.10¼ is 3.10 (the 2 zeros are not shown on the monitor nor in the newspapers). Although they're quite obvious, before doing an example to convert grain price into dollar equivalents to find an average price, I would like to remind you of the following decimal equivalents for fractions: ¼ = .25, ½ = .50, ¾ = .75.

High	Low	Last
$3.10½	$3.09¾	$3.10¼

High	3.1050
Low	3.0975
Last	+ 3.1025

9.3050 ÷ 3 = 3.101666 which rounds off to an average price of 3.1017.

As has been said, the average price may result in a price that's not equal to one of the incremental points of the contract. It doesn't matter. This average price is essential for graphing the direction of the price movements of the contract, and for the % Change figure.

If you are using a monitor or a data retrieval service, grain prices may look like this: 310.2, 310.4 or 310.6. The 2, 4, and 6 designate the fractional cents: $2 = .25 = ¼$, $4 = .50 = ½$, and $6 = .75 = ¾$. Thus, the price of a grain can be expressed in three different ways:

1) $3.10¼ = 3.1025 = 310.2$
2) $3.10½ = 3.1050 = 310.4$
3) $3.10¾ = 3.1075 = 310.6$

Don't let them scare you or confuse you.

There is no point in converting grain prices to total dollars and cents for use in this work. The above conversions will suffice. However, for those of you who prefer converting into money contracts, or are just interested in how it is done, here is how you find the money value. First, you need to know the size of the contract. On the Chicago Board of Trade (CBT), a contract is composed of 5,000 bushels. Now, all you need do is multiply the size of the contracts by the price, and *watch your decimals:* a grain contract selling at 3.10¼ has a dollar value of $15,512.50 (5,000 × 3.1025 = 15,512.50).

C. SOYBEAN OIL

To find the average price for this contract, simply add the high, low and closing price together and divide by 3. There is nothing special to do conversion-wise.

D. SOYBEAN MEAL

To find the dollar value of this contract, just move the decimal point one place to the left. This is how meal prices appear: 192.20, 190.10, 190.30. Using these numbers as the high, low and close, the average price would be found as follows: $19.22 + 19.010 + 19.030 = 57.260 \div 3 = 19.0866666$, which rounds off to 19.087. Multiply this by 1,000, and the money value is $19,087.

E. COCOA

The contract price of cocoa shows the price of 10 tons (contract size) like this: 2.430, 2.402, 2.408. Simply multiply by 1,000 to get the money value. The average price here is $2,413.00.

If at any time you are unsure about how to find any money value, ask your broker. In time, contracts will be traded which are not mentioned in this book. While the principles herein apply to any contract, specifics, as indicated, will have to be known.

Believe me, after trading any commodity for a couple of weeks these computations will be second nature.

Chapter 5

Preparing The
Power Index Graph

Before you even start a graph, you should have accumulated one to two month's worth of data (20 to 40 days). From this material, you will need to determine two pieces of information to set the parameters for the scale of the graph: (1) the size of the daily average price movement during that span of time and (2) the size of the change in the Power Index (Average OI). Using this information, we will then determine what value to assign to each horizontal line so that we have enough space to include the price ranges the contract is likely to exhibit. So the horizontal (left to right) lines will measure the Power Index and the Average Price. The vertical lines are time lines; each vertical line (top to bottom) represents one trading day.

Each graph will have two sections, separated by a horizontal line drawn across the middle of the graph. The top section will be used to measure the Average Price information and the bottom section will be used to measure the Power Index. The Power Index section will also have a horizontal line drawn across it. This line will represent the zero line, which separates positive Adjusted OI figures from negative Adjusted OI figures. Thus, each graph will have two horizontal lines penciled across it when you first start the graph, as illustrated in Figure 7.

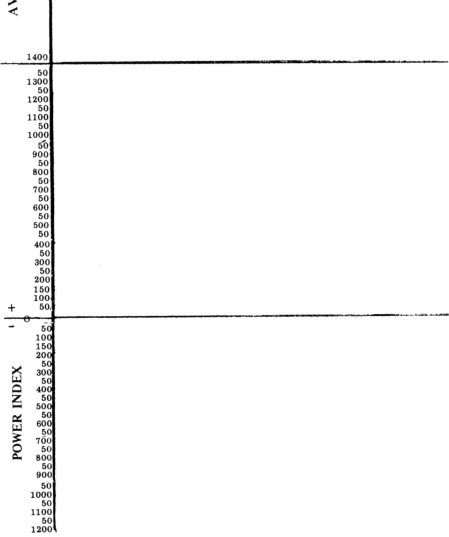

FIGURE 7
JUNE 1984 S&P 500 OPTIONS (CME)

AVERAGE CYCLE

POWER INDEX

+
−

1400
50
1300
50
1200
50
1100
50
1000
50
900
50
800
50
700
50
600
50
500
50
400
50
300
50
200
150
100
50
0
50
100
150
200
50
300
50
400
50
500
50
600
50
700
50
800
50
900
50
1000
50
1100
50
1200

42

On the left side of the graph are two sets of figures, one set for each section of the graph. From the center line moving upward are the values assigned to each horizontal line. These values designate the price increments, per line, for the Average Price information.

The second set of figures apply to the Power Index section. The numbers above the zero line in the Power Index section are designated with a plus (+). They represent positive Adjusted OI and increase in value from the zero line as you move up the scale. The numbers below the zero line are designated with a minus (−). They represent negative Adjusted OI and decrease in value as you move downward from the zero line. This is illustrated on the graph in Figure 7.

At the top of the graph you will write in the name, month and year of the futures contract, followed by the exchange on which the contract is traded, in parentheses. For example, on the graph in Figure 7 you will see at the top: JUNE 1984 S&P 500 (CME).

Let's study the graph, as there are some important lessons to be learned from it. Each line of the Power Index section has a value of 25. How was this value chosen? Checking the 20-day data on the June 1984 S&P 500, and scanning down the Adjusted OI column, I noticed that the change in the Power Index, between days, ranged between 25 and 75 points. So I decided that a value of 25 be applied to each horizontal line. Since the graph is compact and there is very little room to write, I chose to write an increment of 50 on every second line rather than drive myself crazy trying to fit in an increment of 25 on each line. This also makes the graph neater and easier to read.

There is a problem, however. The Power Index (Adjusted OI) shows readings in excess of + 1400, which my graph doesn't show. Notice, too, that there are no negative readings in the Adjusted OI data. Thus, all the negative numbers I have shown on my graph are of no use to us for this contract. That space I took up with negative numbers could have been put to better use on the positive side of the zero line. Which brings up a few important points regarding the placement of the zero line on your graph.

Point 1. The zero line does not have to be equidistant from the center line and the bottom of the graph. The zero line is to be placed in such a way that it best suits the needs of your data.

Point 2. Depending on the contracts you are working with, you may not need a zero line at all!

Suppose, for example, you have been working with the June 84 S&P 500 for about 5 or 6 months and during that time the Power Index, while fluctuating up and down, did not go into minus territory. Now it is early May 1984 and you are preparing to begin graphing the new SEPT 1984 S&P 500. Knowing that the S&P 500 does not exhibit negative Power Index numbers, how do you set up the Power Index section of the graph?

There are two ways to go about it: (1) since previous indicators show no negative Power Index, you can just use the first line at the bottom of the graph as your zero line and denote larger and larger positive increments as you move upward from that point (see Figure 8); or, you can draw in your zero line quite close to the bottom of the graph, just in case you get some negative numbers in the future (see Figure 9).

The reverse would likewise apply if you see that minus Power Index values are the norm. Either avoid drawing in a zero line and use the center line for that purpose, using larger and larger negative numbers as you move down from the center line (see Figure 10); or, you can just drop it down a short distance from the center line, just in case you do get some positive data (see Figure 11).

Returning to our original problem, what do you do if, even after all this careful planning, the Power Index moves into a range you haven't got on your graph? Again, you have a few choices.

In the event your positive Power Index numbers exceed the highest level you have provided for on your graph you can:

44

FIGURE 8
JUNE 1984 S&P 500 OPTIONS (CME)

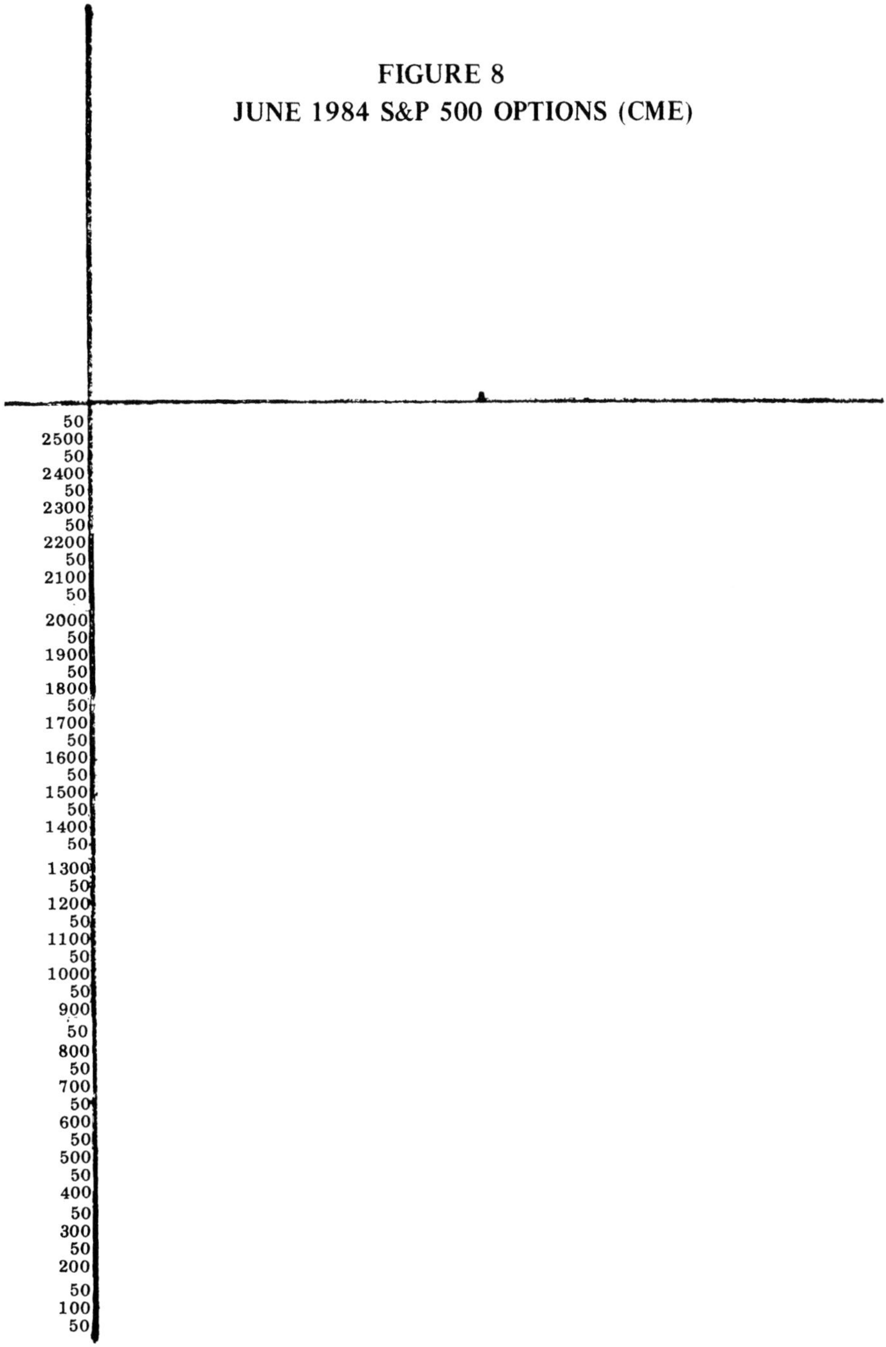

50
2500
50
2400
50
2300
50
2200
50
2100
50

2000
50
1900
50
1800
50
1700
50
1600
50
1500
50
1400
50

1300
50
1200
50
1100
50
1000
50
900
50
800
50
700
50
600
50
500
50
400
50
300
50
200

50
100
50

45

FIGURE 9
JUNE 1984 S&P 500 OPTIONS (CME)

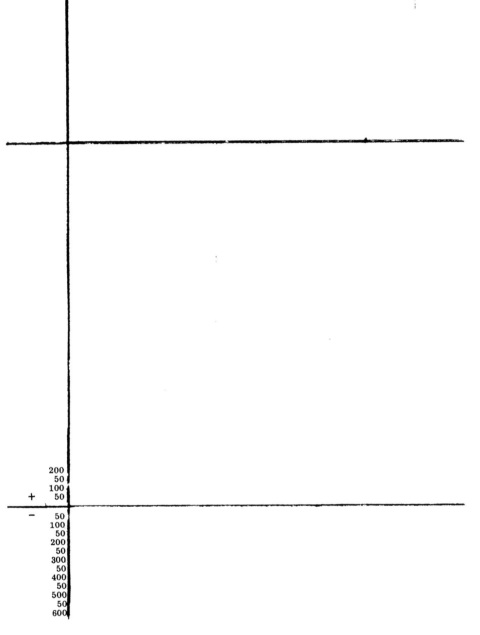

FIGURE 10
JUNE 1984 S&P 500 OPTIONS (CME)

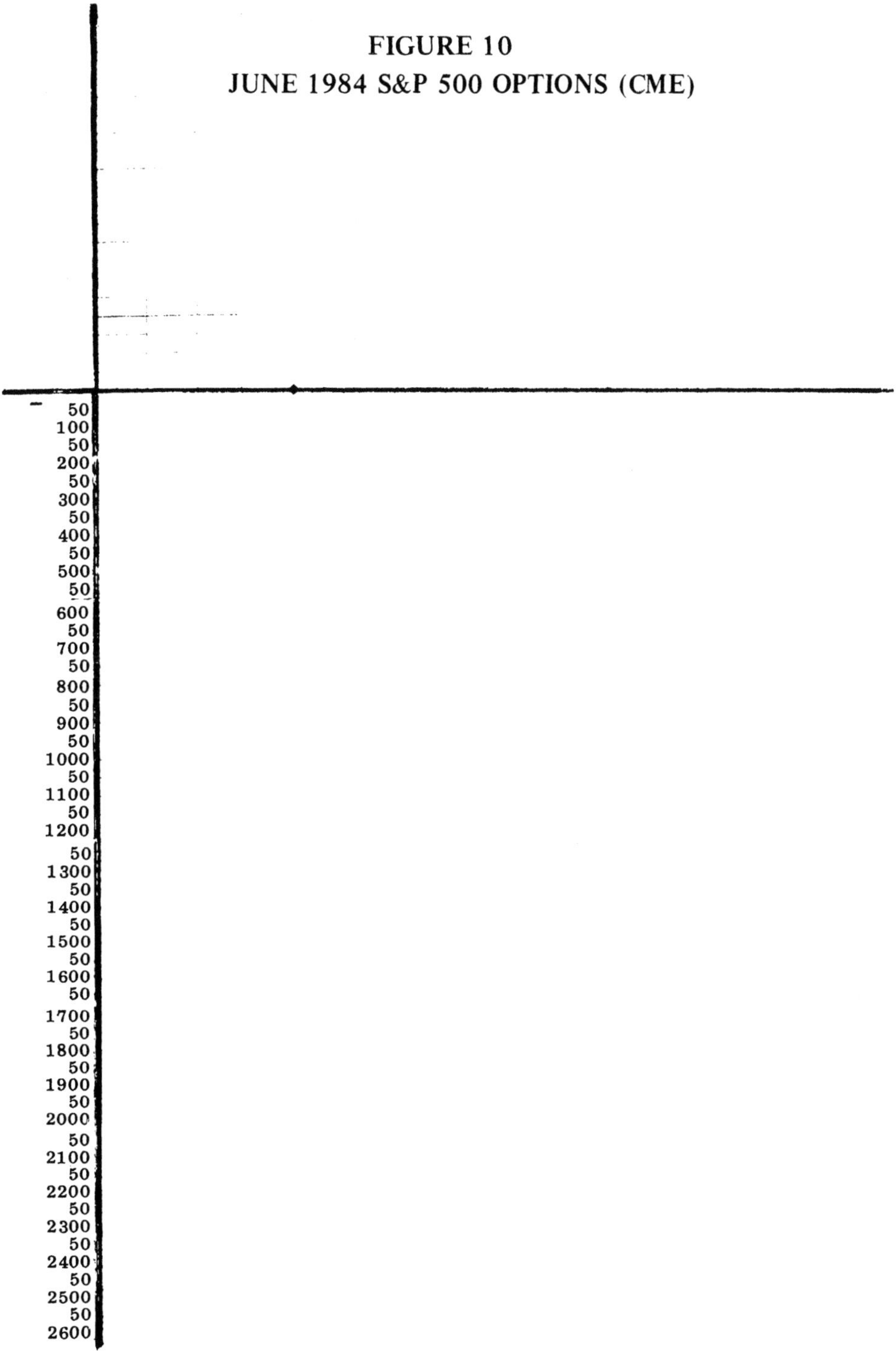

50
100
50
200
50
300
50
400
50
500
50
600
50
700
50
800
50
900
50
1000
50
1100
50
1200
50
1300
50
1400
50
1500
50
1600
50
1700
50
1800
50
1900
50
2000
50
2100
50
2200
50
2300
50
2400
50
2500
50
2600

FIGURE 11
JUNE 1984 S&P 500 OPTIONS (CME)

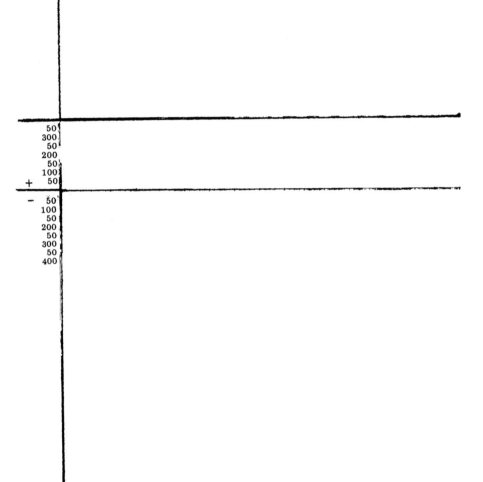

1. Add (in equal increments) higher Power Index values above the center line. This will overlap the Power Index graph onto the Average Price graph. As long as the plotted points for each section don't interfere with each other, this is fine.

2. You can cut the graph in half, along the centerline, and then paste additional graph paper onto the Power Index side (being careful to align the lines and keeping increments equal). This will give you the space to include the additional positive values. Then you can either keep the two graphs separate and simply place one above the other for comparison or paste the Average Price graph onto the Power Index again (above the extension, of course).

In the event your negative Power Index values go below your zero line, just add more graph paper where it is needed.

At this point, you may be thinking that it would be easier to just have two separate pages for each graph. You may be right. I prefer to keep the graphs on the same page for comparison purposes (this will become clear when we discuss tactics and strategies later on). Also, I find there is less opportunity to lose or misplace information when there is less paper to deal with. How you choose to prepare the graphs I'll leave to your own discretion.

The graph paper I use is manufactured by Keuffel & Esser (K&E) Co., ID# 47-1650. You cannot use log or semi-log graph paper. All vertical and horizontal lines must be equidistant. Log and semi-log graph paper does not fit this requirement—the lines are not equidistant. Any size graph paper can be used, providing it adheres to the indicated criteria.

When assigning values to the horizontal lines, it is most important that you keep the increments of each line equal. Each line counts 10 units—this cannot vary. Once you pick a scale, it can't change. If the increment between the first line and the second line on your scale is an increment of 5, the increment between the second line and the third line on your scale must also be 5, and so on. Your scale would show increasing values like so: 5, 10, 15, 20, etc. What you cannot

49

show are increasing values per line like: 5, 12, 17, 23, 25. The increments on your scale must always be equal, in other words, proportionate.

The same rule regarding equal incremental values per line in the Power Index applies with equal force when giving price values to the scale of the Average Price graph. However, while each line must indicate equal increments, you do not and cannot use the same increment for the Average Price scale as you use for the Power Index. Line increments are to be kept consistent *within* each section. Thus, you can choose to employ increments of 20 units per line in the Average Price index (as I did, see the graph in Figure 12), while the scale for the Power Index is in increments of 25.

The same general procedure used to assign line values to the Power Index is also employed for the Average Price. We want to make sure we scale the graph to incorporate the recorded high and low range and also allow sufficient space to include further directional moves in the Average Price. Using the data in Figure 5, we see that the highest high recorded was 168.10 and the lowest low recorded was 155.00, during the 20 trading days. To determine what value to assign per line, add the two values at either end of the range, divide the sum by 2, and then divide that figure by the number of trading days (20 in this instance). This will give you an approximate movement per day in the price data. The arithmetic, for this example, would look like this:

$$168.10 + 155.00 = 323.1 \div 2 = 161.55 \div 20 = 8.08$$

We would round that number off, and use 10-unit increments for the line value. But wait!

The top half is composed of 12 or 13 sections composed of 8 lines each, or at the most, 104 lines. A price move from, say, 155.00 to 156.00, using line increments of 10 points, would take up 10 lines (155.10, 155.20, 155.30...155.90, 156.00). With only 104 lines at our disposal, we would only be able to graph the price range from 155 to 165.4 using 10 point increments (104 lines $\div$ 10 per line = 10.4; 155.00 + 10.4 = 165.4). This

FIGURE 12
JUNE 1984 S&P 500 (CME)

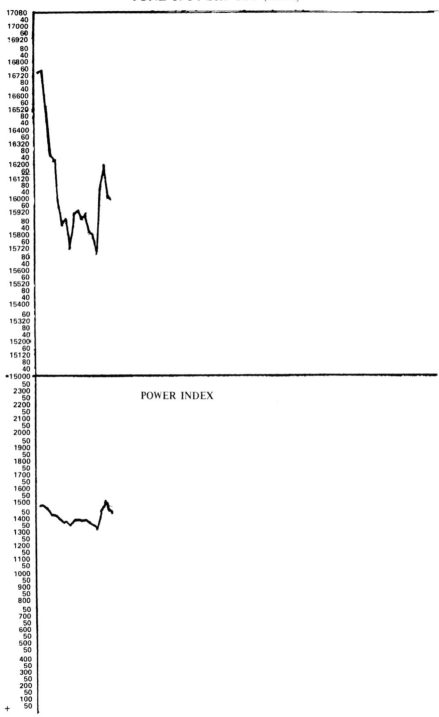

POWER INDEX

would not reach the recorded high of 168.10; also, it would not give us any space for a directional move beyond the recorded high or below the recorded low. We will have to find another line increment.

Since we know our price range is from 155.00 to 168.10, and we also want to leave ourselves room for prices outside those parameters, let's set up our graph to cover a range of 150.00 to 170.00. Every one dollar move in the price of the S&P 500 contract is equal to 100 points. The range we want is a twenty dollar spread (170.00 − 150.00 = 20.00), which is equal to 2,000 points (20 dollars × 100 points = 2,000 points). With 104 lines to work with, we figure out how many points to use per line by dividing the number of lines available into the size of the point spread we want. Thus, we would use line increments of 20, because: 2,000 ÷ 104 = 19.2. This is pretty close to 20, and it is better to use line increments with multiples of 10 or 5—they are easier to visualize. The twenty point increment is what you will see used on the graph in Figure 12, for the Average Price section.

Referring to the same graph, you will see that the Power Index begins at 0 and goes to plus 2400 (number not shown). The Average Price begins at the center line at 150.00 and moves to a top of 170.80, some 270 points above the high of 168.10 recorded during the first three days of February. There are also some 1150 points below the low price of 155.00, so there is plenty of room for price movement.

There is only one other point to address. You can, if your investigation shows a wide move in the Average Price and/or the Power Index, raise or lower the center line to accomodate the movement. Then again, there is always the alternative of putting each graph on its own sheet of graph paper.

This method for finding line values can be applied to any contract.

Chapter 6

Trendlines

GENERAL THOUGHTS ON TRENDLINES

Take any two technicians and ask each one to draw in a trendline on a price graph. The result will probably be A) each one started at a different point and B) each one ended at a different point.

There is no absolute criteria for drawing in a trendline. Only guides can be given in their construction.

Everyone has their own preferences.

TRENDLINE IMPORTANCE

The Power Index method of trading involves trendline use. I'm going to give you the rules I use for trendlines. This will at the very least make it easier for you to interpret my work. At best, you'll learn some new, profitable ideas for trend trading.

This chapter deals with trendline rules. In the next chapter, you'll learn the final rules for using the Power Index. But I felt that the trendline information should be given first. This information can be used on the Power Index—or whatever techniques you may use.

THE FUNCTIONS OF A TRENDLINE

1. Delineate, in bold relief, the increased fear of traders as the trendline edges lower and lower, connecting lower tops in the Power Index.

2. Bring into crystal clarity the acceleration of greed as the T/L edges higher, connecting higher PI low points.

3. Zero in at or near the ingestion of a change in traders' emotions, i.e., fear to greed, greed to fear.

4. An important tool which allows a trader to place worthwhile stops as the PI moves higher and lower.

5. A viable trading trigger, the function of which is to allow a trader to offset and put on trades independent of or in conjunction with the PI.

"Mr. Goldberg, surely you are aware of the fact that a trader who is short a position is happy as it makes lower prices, yet you look upon a falling market as a market of fear. In an upward action, a short position trader suffers, yet you allude to this type of market as one of greed. Would you please explain your insistence at labeling the markets as you do?"

"American traders have a bias toward up moves, and a disdain for down markets. Traders, by and large, trade in anticipation of higher, not lower prices. Therefore, the higher the price the greater the greed. The lower the price, the greater the fear. Thus, I have labeled an up market as one of greed, a down market as one of fear."

CONSTRUCTING A TRENDLINE

The most difficult part of drawing a trendline is in knowing where it should begin. A trendline, like a set of figures, can be manipulated so as to make it literally say or do anything one would desire. Therefore, it is important that you know the correct starting point of a trendline, when it becomes inoperative, and where a new trendline should begin.

We will be studying trendlines covering a 75 day period on the Nov 1985 Soybean contract. A day by day critique of trendlines will be discussed. Scant attention will be paid to the average price work on the graphs. A number of graphs of the same contract comprising different time periods within the 75 day time frame will be used to illustrate various points.

A TRENDLINE HAS LIFE

A trendline is a function of motion. It delineates the direction of the PI, and also the probable direction of the Index. It allows one to trade "off" the line as well as show stop placement. It stands to reason, such a trendline is no ordinary trendline, nor is it drawn in the same manner as conventional trendlines.

THE DIFFERENCE BETWEEN TRENDLINES

Basically, my trading trendline and the conventional trendline are vaguely similar. Both are drawn from upper left to lower right, depicting a declining market, or from lower left to upper right, indicating a rising market. At that point the similarity ends.

A conventional trendline will connect two or three high points. This is a declining market. Its defect lies in the line's distance from present market action. The same can be said for a conventional uptrending line, which cuts across two or three low points in an upwardly direction. Here, too, the same defect is present.

A conventional trendline cannot give a trader data on where to place stops. Further, because it tends to be distant from present action, due to the angle it is drawn from the top (bottom) two or three points, it is incapable of triggering trading signals until a move has travelled some distance toward the outer reaches of the line's descent or ascent. So much for conventional trendlines. As we go from day to day in our trendline work, you will see how a trendline should be drawn, and the positive trading results emanating from its correct construction.

WHERE TO START A TRENDLINE

When possible, a trendline should begin from the first day you started to graph the futures contract. This is not always practical. If the second or third day's high is higher (or lower) than the high of day one, you may or may not have the beginning of a trendline. Conversely, the first few days depicting lows may see a low lower than the previous low, or a combination of lows moving up and down so as to make it impossible to draw a trendline from day one.

In time, usually within the first 10 days of graphing, the highs may begin to make lower highs, as the ensuing rallies fail to better the previous rally. Start the trendline from the highest high during that period and begin connecting the subsequent lower highs. Apply this procedure in reverse, of course, as you connect the higher lows.

A TRENDLINE FAILURE

You've drawn a beautiful down-sloping trendline for a period of five weeks. From the last high at which the line touches, the subsequent PI action becomes exasperating. Instead of the PI making lower highs, a sideways action begins. The PI is forming a trading range at which the rallies are about the same height and the reactions (lows) reach a point, which they bounce off. A stalemate. No new highs, no new lows.

The horizontal area is what I call an "emotional area of change." Emotions of fear and greed tend to build up or change over time. They do not change "on a dime," so to speak. However, once the dominant emotion manifests itself, it is reflected in the direction of the PI.

The trendline touching the last high (low) point prior to the "emotional area of change," should be discarded and a new line drawn when the PI asserts itself once again. If you have an open position during the tug of war between fear and greed, refer to the chapter on trading tactics as to the course of action to take.

The tug of emotions may result (usually will) in one of three outcomes:

1. The Power Index may continue its see-saw action until expiration of the contract, admittedly an unlikely situation. See "Trading Tactics" for the course of action to take in this situation.

2. The Power Index may break to the upside.

3. The Power Index may penetrate the low end of the range.

Refer to the trading tactics section to learn what to do in any of these eventualities.

TRENDLINE FIGURES

Figure 13. The PI and AI action covering a 75 day trading period from Feb. 21, 1985 and ending June 7, 1985.
(Actual data shown in Figure 15).

Line A-AI shows a trendline which became inoperative due to a subsequent sideways action. Had you offset your long (see Point A, where you would have initiated the trade) and gone short you would have had ample opportunity to offset with a small profit.

Line B-BI is the prelude to a major sell-off in beans.

FIGURE 13

THE POWER INDEX COMPARED WITH AVERAGE PRICE

58

Figure 14. Two trendlines are shown. Line A is a trendline which branches out and away from the immediate trading action, rendering it useless for putting on or taking off positions. This graph begins on Day 41 and culminates on Day 75. (Actual data shown in Figure 15).

The second trendline (B) is the correct way to draw a trend. It virtually hugs the trading action. Notice, too, Point C, where an offsetting and reverse signal took place, many hundreds of dollars away from the conventional (Line A) trendline.

Note: Different PI scales are used to show a particular lesson in a clear vein.

FIGURE 14
THE CORRECT WAY TO DRAW A TRENDLINE

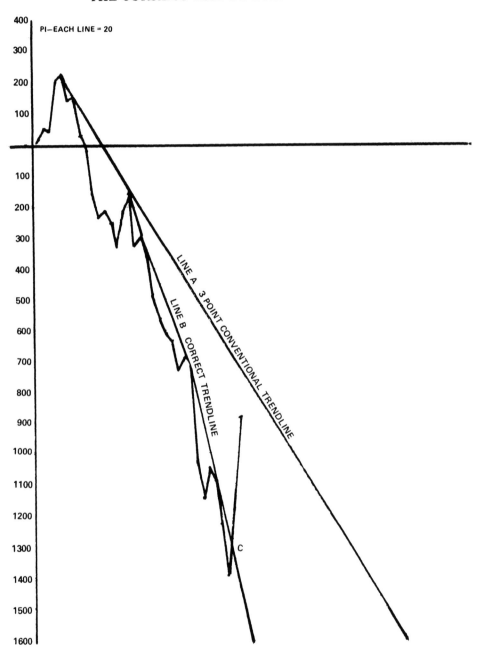

FIGURE 15
NOV 1985 SOYBEANS

2/21/85

DAY	HIGH	LOW	CLOSE	AVG.PR.	% CHGE.	OPEN INT.	ADJ. OI
1	607.00	600.50	605.25	604.25	---	---	---
2	604.00	600.00	600.75	601.58	- .44	8,781	- 39
3	595.00	586.00	590.75	590.58	- 1.83	8,999	- 204
4	596.00	589.50	593.25	592.92	+ .40	9,067	- 168
5	598.50	591.00	592.75	594.08	+ .20	8,742	- 151
6	592.50	588.50	588.75	589.92	- .70	8,928	- 213
7	592.50	589.00	591.50	591.00	+ .18	9,127	- 197
8	591.50	584.00	588.00	587.83	- .54	9,123	- 246
9	588.00	583.50	587.00	586.17	- .28	9,182	- 272
10	590.00	586.50	586.75	587.75	+ .27	9,291	- 247
11	589.75	585.50	589.25	588.17	+ . 7	9,087	- 241
12	597.50	589.00	592.50	593.00	+ .82	8,891	- 168
13	596.00	593.00	594.75	594.58	+ .27	9,024	- 144
14	595.00	591.75	591.75	592.83	- .29	9,234	- 171
15	597.00	591.50	593.75	594.08	+ .21	9,244	- 152
16	599.00	592.50	597.25	596.25	+ .37	9,430	- 117
17	600.00	596.00	596.25	595.92	- . 5	9,446	- 122
18	605.00	598.00	603.75	602.25	+ 1.06	9,702	- 19
19	620.50	608.50	619.00	616.00	+ 2.28	9,844	+ 205
20	616.75	611.00	612.50	613.42	- .42	10,122	+ 163
21	620.00	612.25	613.75	615.33	+ .31	10,240	+ 195
22	613.75	608.75	610.25	610.92	- .72	10,345	+ 121
23	610.50	606.25	608.25	608.33	- .42	10,080	+ 79
24	612.50	608.25	610.00	610 25	+ .32	9,739	+ 110
25	618.00	613.00	613.50	614.83	+ .75	10,429	+ 188
26	613.75	609.25	613.75	612.25	- .42	9,834	+ 147
27	616.00	610.50	612.25	612.92	+ .11	10,131	+ 158
28	609.50	605.00	605.25	606.58	- 1.03	10,060	+ 54
29	606.00	603.00	605.50	604.83	- .29	9,938	+ 25
30	608.00	603.75	606.00	605.92	- .18	9,585	+ 8
31	609.50	603.25	609.00	607.25	+ .22	9,696	+ 29
32	616.50	608.00	616.25	613.58	+ 1.04	9,816	+ 131
33	620.50	613.50	613.75	615.92	+ .38	9,747	+ 168
34	618.00	610.50	612.00	613.50	- .39	9,931	+ 129
35	617.00	614.75	615.25	615.67	+ .35	9,874	+ 164
36	618.75	609.50	609.75	612.67	- .49	10,028	+ 115
37	612.50	604.75	606.50	607.92	- .78	10,080	+ 36
38	608.75	604.50	606.25	606.50	- .23	9,988	+ 13
39	608.50	602.00	604.00	604.83	- .28	9,950	- 15
40	608.75	605.25	608.00	607.33	+ .41	10,196	+ 27

FIGURE 15
NOV 1985 SOYBEANS (CONT'D)

DAY	HIGH	LOW	CLOSE	AVG.PR.	% CHGE.	OPEN INT.	ADJ. OI
41	608.50	604.00	607.75	606.75	- .10	10,129	+ 17
42	611.50	606.50	609.25	609.08	+ .38	10,160	+ 56
43	610.00	606.00	609.25	608.42	- .11	10,505	+ 44
44	623.00	609.50	621.00	617.83	+ 1.55	10,222	+ 202
45	622.75	617.00	617.50	619.08	+ .20	10,632	+ 223
46	617.00	613.00	613.50	614.50	- .74	11,037	+ 141
47	618.75	611.00	615.25.	615.00	+ .08	11,171	+ 150
48	615.00	603.50	607.25	608.58	- 1.04	11,664	+ 29
49	609.00	604.75	606.00	606.58	- .33	11,176	- 8
50	605.00	595.00	597.75	599.25	- 1.21	11,294	- 145
51	599.25	592.50	592.75	594.83	- .74	11,755	- 232
52	598.00	591.25	597.75	595.67	+ .14	12,030	- 215
53	600.00	589.50	591.75	593.75	- .32	12,061	- 254
54	592.00	587.50	590.75	590.08	- .62	12,403	- 331
55	598.25	592.25	595.75	595.42	+ .90	13,071	- 213
56	599.00	595.75	598.75	597.83	+ .40	13,654	- 158
57	597.00	586.00	589.50	590.83	- 1.17	14,274	- 325
58	592.50	588.75	592.00	591.08	+ .04	14,563	- 319
59	594.00	586.00	586.75	588.92	- .37	14,423	- 372
60	587.75	582.75	583.25	584.58	- .74	14,704	- 481
61	585.75	578.50	580.25	581.50	- .53	14,891	- 560
62	582.50	575.75	580.50	579.58	- .33	14,626	- 608
63	583.75	575.50	576.25	578.50	- .19	14,784	- 636
64	577.75	571.00	576.00	574.92	- .62	14,861	- 728
65	577.75	574.25	577.25	576.42	+ .26	14,728	- 689
66	577.50	573.75	574.75	575.33	- .19	15,080	- 718
67	571.00	560.50	.560.75	564.08	- 1.96	15,506	- 1022
68	563.25	557.50	558.75	559.83	- .75	15,953	- 1142
69	577.75	554.00	557.25	563.00	+ .57	16,948	- 1045
70	564.50	558.50	562.00	561.67	- .24	17,468	- 1087
71	562.00	554.50	554.75	557.08	- .82	17,321	- 1229
72	554.25	549.50	552.25	552.00	- .91	17,943	- 1392
73	561.00	553.50	560.75	558.42	+ 1.16	18,094	- 1182
74	570.00	563.50	569.50	567.67	+ 1.66	18,154	- 881
75	589.75	571.00	585.25	582.00	+ 2.52	18,536	- 414

Trading Rules And Tactics

Any trading tactics must be based, in part on the proposition that feelings, intuition, call it what you will, enter into a trader's decisions. To some degree, we all have intuition. I sincerely believe that, through training, the subconscious mind can become receptive to thought and visual impulses, which will at some point in time alert (intuition at work) the trader to a piece of data he may have overlooked while scanning the Power Index line.

Toward that end, I have included numerous graphs, each detailing one or two points dealing with the Power Index and Average Price. It is believed that, by breaking down points, individually or in twos, the ability to interpret the Power Index and the Average Price will be enhanced. This, in turn, will add to the store of knowledge in the subconscious mind, which, by extension, will sharpen the intuitive process. For this exercise, I have chosen the June 1984 S&P 500 futures contract.

First, let me say that this is just because I know traders. You'll want to apply your intuition. And your own rules. I don't doubt that. I'll give you trading rules. At the start, you'll think they're more valuable than this subconscious instinct. But once you start "experimenting," you'll find this discussion invaluable.

The Power Index work forms and illustrative graphs for the

period covered are included at the end of this chapter. The time period is from January 26, 1984 up to and including April 19, 1984. The graph in Figure 13 will show the movement of the Power Index and the Average Price over that span of time.

Figure 13 does not include notations or trendlines. All you will see are the Power Index and Average Price. The subsequent figures will highlight factors which I will bring to your attention, one or two points in each figure. This way you can absorb everything one rule at a time. Data used in this study and for all contracts are from *The Wall Street Journal.* The time frame used in this study is 60 days.

Before studying strategy, tactics and the figures, let us first take a look at the Power Index work form. I have included all eight columns so as to make it easier for you to refer to particular days. Now, let's assume you've not worked with the S&P 500 in the past.

Look at Feb. 6th and 9th. Notice the large change in the open interest from the days prior to each of those dates. Was either day a misprint? No, on the following day, the open interest was close to (actually above) the open interest amount for each of those days. We could have said that as far as the S&P 500 is concerned, open interest figures can fluctuate between 400-to-600-point moves a day.

On Feb. 24th, we see that the OI increased by almost 1,000. On Mar. 7th, by 1,200, and on Mar. 13th by almost 4,000! Between Mar. 14th and 15th, another 4,000. We can throw away our earlier assumption about a 400-600 change in the OI as being normal. Now, we can conclude that this contract is capable of an OI change in excess of 4,000. If we notice a larger change, then we can check for an OI error.

On March 5th, a funny thing happened. *The Wall Street Journal* indicated the OI at 1616, obviously an error. I changed the amount to 7616. Why? That is close to the average OI for the last few days. In addition, on the following day (3/6/84) the OI stood at 8255. Errors will be made. When you work with these numbers, watch out for misprints in prices and open interest.

Something else to watch out for. The Power Index will alert you to a seeming contradiction. One in which the Power Index moves one way with the Average Price moving in the opposite direction. It is, therefore, important that you study your Power Index graph, paying particular attention to the direction of the Power Index (Adjusted OI), as opposed to the direction of the Average Price. This is because the Power Index is the primary index used to determine when to put on a trade. Why? Because the Power Index ("PI") measures fear and fear moves the price. Price does not move the emotion.

On Jan. 27th, (* on work form) the Average Price for the June 84 S&P 500 index contract stood at 168.20. The PI stood at +1209. On Mar. 19, the index price as at 162.47 and notice, the PI (Adjusted OI) was +1688(!); or, higher by 479.

When the Power Index rises or falls and the Average Price does not move appreciably in the same direction—*watch out!* Within a few weeks, the Average Price will rise or fall dramatically. The question then becomes, "Which way is the Average Price going to move?"

When the Power Index rises without a corresponding increase in the Average Price, it means that the contract is being shorted and that prices will soon drop. On April 11, the S&P 500 was at 156.92, or 555 points below its March 19 price of 162.47!

The Power Index ("PI") and Average Price ("AP") do not necessarily move together, and they do not tell us anything on a percentage move basis. What they do tell us is:

1. If the PI moves higher and the AP also moves higher, proportionally, there will be an increase in prices.

2. If the PI moves lower and the AP also moves lower, proportionally, there will be a decrease in prices.

3. If the PI moves in one direction and the AP does not move along with it appreciably it denotes a non-confirmation of the existing price trend. The price will move up or down, depending on the PI, within the next couple of weeks.

Situation 1 indicates a signal to offset a short position and go long. Situation 2 suggests a trader should go short and/or offset a long position. Situation 3 is a false signal. The Average Price did not confirm the PI to put on or offset a position.

A movement in the PI is a result of increased or decreased open interest. Open interest, you will remember, is a measure of the number of contracts currently being traded in the market. Strength in the market is denoted by rising prices, which are the result of new longs entering the market in anticipation of higher prices. Weakness in the market is caused by longs pulling out of their positions for fear of falling prices. This drives the price down. When old longs get tired of their position and start to sell off, the price on the Exchange tends to lower somewhat. As a result, the short sellers, who enter market orders as a rule, will complete their trades more easily. Thus, most of the new interest in the market is negative. This weakens the price structure.

When the Power Index rises and there is not a corresponding rise in the Average Price, it indicates the underlying effect of the market is weakness, not strength. Strength in the market is shown by rising prices. A long who gets out of a position obviously does not think the price is going any higher. A short seller who enters the market agrees with that opinion. The opinions of these traders weaken the price structure, so while the open interest will show an increase in trading, the increased interest it registers is of a negative nature. This is proven by the price of the contract; the lack of a positive response (no up move) to the interest taken in it. During the next couple of weeks, the price will fall.

If the Power Index falls sharply, and there is not a corresponding drop in the Average Price, this means that new longs are entering the market and offsetting the short open interest. A reversal of trend is going to take place in the next couple of weeks, and the price will move higher.

Make a mental note that when there is a divergence between the Power Index and the Average Price, a change will usually take place within a couple of weeks. Consider going out of your position within that time span if the PI anticipates a move against your position.

At this point, a note on stop orders will give the above information more meaning. When the PI is rising in concert with the AP and you have a short position, *lower* your mental stop. The price is about to move against you. Stops are mental and not actual. This means that, while you have written down a stop (preferably on the graph), they are only given to your AE when they are hit on the close, at which time instruct your AE to sell out the position using a "market order."

If the Power Index is falling and the Average Price is moving sideways, it means that shorts are covering. The PI is falling because traders are reducing the open interest measurements. Since the price is not moving, we can conclude that the traders leaving the market are the shorts. The price will work its way higher within 10 days or so. When the PI turns up, look to buy a contract.

Sideways movement that develops after a long decline or a long upmove indicates a probable reversal of the previous trend. At that time, watch your PI very closely. When it changes direction, put on a position in line with the new direction of the PI.

Occasionally, the sideways action is simply a pause to refresh and the previous move will continue. However, this is the exception to the rule. You can assume that sideways action denotes the heralding of a reversal of the previous trend and upon confirmation of the PI, put on the appropriate trade. If the PI moves lower for weeks on end and you are short, be prepared to immediately offset when the PI turns up. The reverse is also true. When an uptrending PI reverses, get rid of your long position and prepare to short the contract.

To this point in time, I have put greatest focus on the Power Index, mentioning the Average Price only in its importance relative to the PI. The Average price is significant because it filters out the daily trading. It is designed to give a better handle on the strength or weakness of the price structure. This, when used in tandem with the Power Index (Adjusted OI), gives you a powerful tool toward profitably trading futures contracts.

Rigidity kills, flexibility saves. As you gain experience working with the AP and PI, your sixth sense (intuition) will alert you to possible impending changes in the direction of the contract's price, allowing you to pay particular attention to a special contract.

While we will be discussing this technique in greater detail when we study the graphs, I just wanted to bring it to your attention at this time. Say you have been tracking the Average Price and Power Index for a few months. Your graph shows a downsloping trendline, which over the past three weeks has tended toward the horizontal. This suggests that the Average Price and/or the Power Index has stopped falling and may be in the process of bottoming out. A downsloping trendline is one which moves from upper left to lower right, connecting the tops, or the rallies, in either the PI or AP. An unsloping trendline is one which moves from lower left to upper right, disconnecting the retractions, or bottoms, of either the PI or AP. Each low is a little higher in an upward trend. Each high is a little lower in a downward trend.

The second thing you notice is that the contract moves lower for twelve to sixteen days, then rallies, then moves lower, then rallies for a few days, etc. Then you notice that the AP and/or PI for the last few weeks has not moved dramatically. Now we are at the 16th to 19th day with the contract's price. The AP and the PI are doing nothing. What can you expect to happen next and what action should you take?

1. Sideways action may continue indefinitely. If you are out of the position, stay out.

2. The price breaks down. Go short. (See Figure 18).

3. The price breaks, but there is no confirmation on the Power Index. This suggests that longs in the contract are getting out, and that new shorting is minimal. The trendline is

pointing sharply to the downside and the duration of this downmove is exceeding previous moves. Experience tells me that this has all the earmarks of a wash-out (the final thrust down). The reason: a non-confirmation, a much steeper trendline break and a longer time in the present move than previously. When you see this type of action, you will know that a change in trend will soon take place.

The longer a trend is in effect, the closer it is to a reversal. Some of the signs of a trend reversal from down to up are: sharp breaks in the price to the downside and a steep downsloping trendline connecting the tops. A reversal from an uptrend to a downtrend is indicated by sharp moves to the upside in either the PI or AP, coupled with a very steep upsloping trendline. This indicates that a blow-off is due. The final stretch is taking place in preparation for a reversal in trend to the downside. A frothy top is one where there is a lot of action but little price movement. This can be seen by the PI moving either higher or lower dramatically without a related move in the AP itself.

4. When, after the plunge, the Power Index turns up, go long. After a rise, when the Power Index turns down, go short.

5. When the trendline is penetrated, you can safely go long— especially if the average time the contract has been declining is longer than its recent norm.

Go in at a specific price, go out at the market. The second part of this rule is, *never, but absolutely never, be compromised.* Obviously, when a mental stop is hit, the market has reversed direction and you must immediately get out of your position. You do this by instructing your AE to write a market order. When this order hits the floor of the Exchange, it will be immediately executed at the best available price.

Protect your capital and protect your profits. Don't chisel for a better price. When your stop is hit, you run like hell! There are no ifs, ands or buts. You offset at the market.

Going into a trade allows you some latitude. Call your AE and instruct him to call the floor of the Exchange for a quote, or ask him to check his price monitor for the last price at which the contract traded.

The rules herein apply with slight modification to all contracts. So study them. They are few in number. Their importance, with respect to keeping losses down and increasing profit potential, are inestimable.

Before we begin our study of the S&P 500 graphs, there is a final point I want to bring to your attention. The graphs comprise a 3 month time span (60 - 70 trading days). Since a longer graph is difficult to use for training purposes, I decided on the 3 month period. Keep in mind that you would simply be seeing more of the same information repeated. This way we can zero in with less distraction, using a shorter time frame.

All figures use a 20 point per line price value for the AP and a 10 point per line value for the PI. To make it easier to follow, when referring to the figure, you will notice that I have written in multiples of 80 points on the AP and 40 point intervals on the PI. On the top of the graph I have noted the point per line value for the AP. It is a good idea to incorporate this into your own work. It's too easy to rush through a graph and make posting errors because you thought you knew the line values.

If you have ever seen a blueprint for a house or a schematic of the wiring for said house, you would be looking at a maze of lines. Each of these lines convey a message: the length and thickness of the lumber; the size, length, and type of wire; where the connections are made; and the type of joints to use. The lines on the PI and AP graphs, and their relationship, convey important messages as well. At different junctures along the way, the movement of the Power Index and Average Price alert us to important points and take on different meanings, as we have discussed, and which will be elaborated.

Please turn to Figure 16. The top half shows how the S&P 500 performed price-wise. The bottom section illustrates the movement of the Power Index. Clearly, what you are seeing is a total and unmitigated selling off of the S&P 500 index. Not in the AP graph, but in the Power Index. What this portends is a down S&P index, a falling stock market and an opportunity to become wealthy trading the June S&P 500 index. I am going to review the overall picture and the individual particulars. Subsequent figures will highlight what I am saying.

In explaining Figure 16, I will refer to the number of days. Each vertical line represents one day. Follow along as best you can. Keep in mind that the salient points will be covered with many more examples throughout this book.

I. Overview—Average Price

During the 60-day period, the S&P 500 Average Price was moving in a range of about 500 points. This occurred after it broke down during the first 13 days, from about the 168.50 area to the 157.30 area. Assume you had sold short at 168.00 during the first five days. Should you offset? Yes and no. Had you offset at about 159.00, which occurred between the 13th and 15th day, your profit would have been 900 points, or thereabouts, or $4,500. All this profit in about two and a half weeks. Not a bad move.

The PI indicates the probable price direction, so act on the indications of the Power Index because it will invariably precede price movement. Remember, *fear* moves prices and the PI measures the fear and emotions of the traders—the power behind the market.

It is easy to be a quarterback after the game. How nicely I described what you should have done *after* the fact. Well, let's see what the Power Index, your key to wealth, was saying.

II. Overview—Power Index

The Power Index was screaming: "Go short" during the last 21 days on the graph. The PI was making lower tops and lower lows. This means weakness in the price structure, which interests the shorts and bothers the longs. Lower tops and lower lows indicate distribution of the contract itself and/or price weakness. This portends lower prices—people are getting out of their long positions and shorts are increasing their net short positions in the contract.

Look at the highest top (the first one on Day 38) of the PI. See it? Good. During the previous 10 days, the PI rallied to the aforementioned top, but, and this is a critical but, the rally in the Average Price reversed! Another non-confirmation. The PI made its highest top at that point. If buyers were more interested than shorts, the price would have moved much higher, which it did not. The Power Index was higher at 162.80 than during the past 7 weeks, when the Average Price was higher by about 600 points. What this means is that longs in the contract were tired and wanted out. The PI was saying, in its dramatic move up from a low of about 1000 to 1688, that this rally was false and wouldn't last. Whenever you see this type of pattern: a sharp PI spike up with a mediocre rise in the AP, the rally is not to be trusted.

So what happened on the 45th day, when the PI fell out of bed for the remainder of the 60 days, while at the same time the reaction was nothing to write home about? Short net position holders in the contract were getting tired of a do-nothing contract. Many of them had substantial profits from the first week, and now they wanted out. The AP and PI subsequently rallied. Then, during the last five days, both the AP and PI could not go through their previous highs.

Notice, too, that the Average Price during the last 10 days found support near previous lows, but the PI made a new low! This means some new shorts came into the market (new PI lows). Based on everything I've said up to now, a new down leg in the S&P 500, the Dow and the market as a whole should begin here.

Let's return once again to the Average Price section. Look at the lows. On average, the AP makes a low, then rallies every 10 to 12 days. Now, study the action for the last two days of the figure. A downward move has begun. It will last at least another 5 to 7 days, which will take it out 10 to 12 days away from the previous low. How far it will move is hard to say. However, the lower lows in the PI signal a penetration of the support prices (previous lows) on the Average Price line.

What are you, a futures trader, to do? When you see a spike up in the PI without a corresponding upward thrust in the AP, you know the rally is false. You go short! The non-confirmation shows the prices will weaken.

Stop Loss Orders

Probably the most difficult decision to implement is to place your stop loss order. Let's approach this most important tactic using the Power Index. The Average Price closest to the spike in the PI occurred the day before at about 162.80. Let's assume that, after studying this book, you shorted a June contract at 162.00.

During the following few weeks, you would have been quite happy, since the Average Price was making lower tops and the Power Index lower bottoms. A most bearish scenario.

Figure 17 is going to show you a trendline covering the last 24 days of the Power Index. Carefully study how I have drawn it in. Near each top is a letter: A, B, and C. These letters show how the trendline changes its angle of descent. A trendline, to be effective, must connect one top to the next top. Since tops or bottoms, for that matter, are rarely precise, you have to adjust for that angle variation. Figure 18 will show the sideways action of the average price. The previous chapter described this trendline construction in detail.

The two horizontal lines in the Average Price section in Figure 18 delineate the trading range. A trading range is the range of prices within which the contract has traded during a period of time. The previous high points and low points will be within these parameters. A false rally or reaction penetrates the upper or lower boundaries of the trading range. It's false because within 1 or 2 days the price will fall back into the range and continue within those boundaries. There are times when the trading range is penetrated, either up or down, and the prices continue in this new direction. This will usually be seen within the next 3 days. What happens is that the price penetrates the range, then falls back, and then takes off in a new direction.

Figure 19 indicates how you can approximate the date that a probable low is expected. Under no circumstances are you to put on a trade in anticipation of an impending price trough. Not to heed this advice is to court danger. Danger, in this business, is losses. Let the PI signals be your guide to profitable trading. *Not The Prices.*

I include Figure 19, with further explanatory material, to nourish your subconscious mind. As you evaluate this work further, you will intuitively make note of the duration of the PI and AP trends. Usually, I will jot down on the graph the approximate date that a turn should be expected. This should be another point in your visual and mental evaluative process in trading futures.

There are 4 points, or bottoms, from which a rally of some proportion commenced. Between point 1 and point 2, 7 days elapsed. Eleven days between points 2 and 3, 9 days between points 3 and 4, and 14 days between points 4 and 5. To obtain the average number of days between the two lows, you simply add the number of days in all the cycles and divide the total by the number of figures used to obtain that total. Four sets of numbers, composed of 7, 11, 9, and 14 days, total to 41 days. Dividing by 4 gives an approximate interval between lows of 10.25 days. This can be rounded off to 10 days, plus or minus 2 days.

We then can expect a low in the June 84 S&P 500 to occur every 9 to 11 days. But wait. We might want to know how to predict the intermediate lows, rather than the short term lows. To find the intermediate lows, we will use point 1 to point 3 and point 3 to point 5, and see what we get. There are 18 days between the first two points and 23 days between the second two. Adding those numbers and dividing by 2 will give us our intermediate time frame. This tells us when a significant low is due.

$18 + 23 = 41 \div 2 = 20.5$ days, rounded off to 21 days. The more points you use, the higher the reliability that a significant low will occur within two or three days of the time predicted. This is certainly something to keep in mind.

FIGURE 16
THE POWER INDEX APPLIED TO S&P 500 OPTIONS

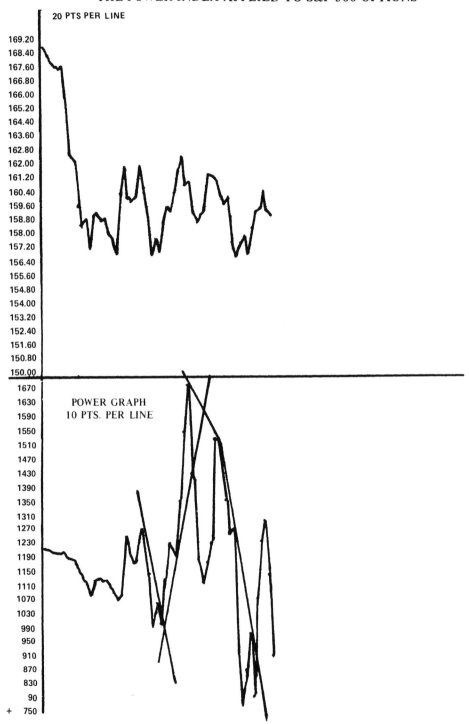

20 PTS PER LINE

POWER GRAPH
10 PTS. PER LINE

FIGURE 17
THE POWER INDEX TRENDLINE

POWER INDEX LAST 24 DAYS OF 60 DAY TIME FRAME

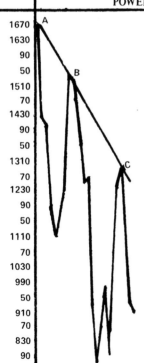

77

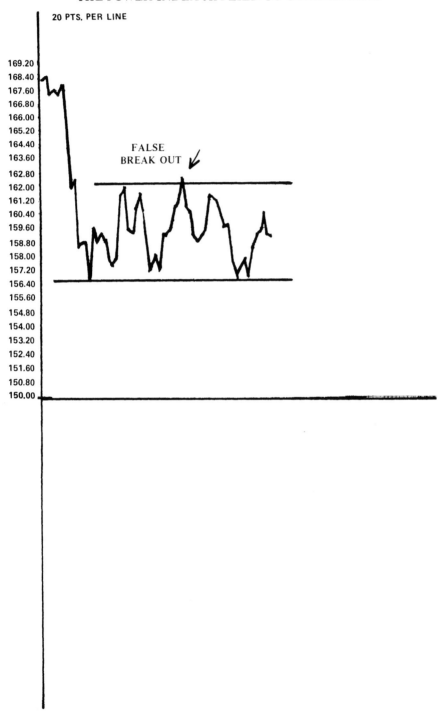

FIGURE 18
THE POWER INDEX APPLIED TO CONGESTIONS

20 PTS. PER LINE

FALSE
BREAK OUT

78

FIGURE 19
APPROXIMATING THE DATE OF THE NEXT PROBABLE LOW

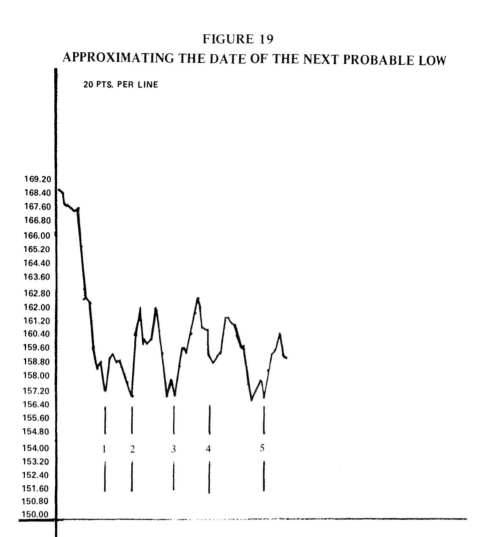

FIGURE 20
JUNE 1984 S&P 500

DATE	HIGH	LOW	CLOSE	AVG.PR.	% CHGE.	OPEN INT.	ADJ. OI
1/26/84	169.50	168.15	168.25	168.63	---	1,212	+ 1212
27	168.70	167.45	168.45	168.20	- .0025	1,279	+ 1209*
30	169.05	166.90	167.40	167.78	- .0025	1,390	+ 1206
31	168.20	166.90	167.65	167.58	- .0012	1,372	+ 1204
2/ 1	168.10	166.85	167.30	167.42	- .0010	1,478	+ 1203
2	168.10	166.85	167.85	167.60	+ .0011	1,491	+ 1205
3	168.10	163.95	164.20	165.42	- .0130	1,524	+ 1185
6	163.80	161.80	161.90	162.50	- .0005	* 1,988	+ 1184
7	163.10	161.15	162.35	162.20	- .0018	2,199	+ 1180
8	162.60	158.20	158.50	159.77	- .0150	2,280	+ 1146
9	159.75	157.05	158.70	158.50	- .0079	2,492	+ 1126
10	159.40	158.40	158.80	158.87	- .0023	* 3,084	+ 1119
13	158.85	156.20	156.60	157.22	- .0104	3,462	+ 1083
14	159.75	157.85	159.60	159.07	+ .0118	3,552	+ 1125
15	160.50	158.60	158.80	159.30	+ .0014	3,708	+ 1130
16	159.45	158.00	159.25	158.90	- .0025	4,196	+ 1120
17	159.75	158.40	158.80	158.98	+ .0005	4,479	+ 1122
21	159.20	157.55	157.80	158.18	- .0050	4,455	+ 1100
22	158.75	157.15	157.40	157.77	- .0026	4,716	+ 1088
23	158.05	155.00	157.85	156.97	- .0051	4,783	+ 1064
24	161.55	158.10	161.45	160.37	+ .0217	* 5,767	+ 1189
27	163.35	160.40	161.90	161.88	+ .0094	6,136	+ 1247
28	161.60	159.35	159.50	160.15	- .0107	6,106	+ 1182
29	161.50	158.90	159.30	159.90	- .0016	7,068	+ 1171
3/ 1	161.05	158.65	160.75	160.15	+ .0016	7,293	+ 1183
2	162.85	161.25	161.60	161.90	+ .0109	7,861	+ 1269
5	161.40	160.00	160.55	160.65	- .0077	**7,616	+ 1210
6	161.20	158.30	158.35	159.28	- .0085	8,255	+ 1140
7	157.60	156.05	157.10	156.92	- .0148	* 9,451	+ 1000
8	158.85	156.70	157.90	157.82	+ .0057	10,181	+ 1058
9	157.80	156.20	157.10	157.03	- .0050	11,261	+ 1002
12	159.35	157.35	159.20	158.63	+ .0102	12,162	+ 1126
13	160.85	158.80	159.15	159.60	+ .0061	*16,145	+ 1224
14	160.30	158.30	159.55	159.38	- .0014	19,385	+ 1197
15	161.10	159.45	160.70	160.42	+ .0065	23,498	+ 1350
16	162.75	160.90	161.30	161.65	+ .0077	26,472	+ 1554
19	163.00	161.85	162.55	162.47	+ .0051	26,201	+ 1688*
20	161.75	159.90	160.80	160.82	- .0102	25,533	+ 1428
21	161.40	160.20	160.45	160.68	- .0009	25,340	+ 1405

80

FIGURE 20 (CONT'D)
JUNE 1984 S&P 500

DATE	HIGH	LOW	CLOSE	AVG.PR.	% CHGE.	OPEN INT.	ADJ. OI
3/22/84	160.05	158.75	159.10	159.30	- .0086	25,263	+ 1188
23	159.50	158.10	158.95	158.85	- .0028	25,260	+ 1117
26	159.90	158.65	159.05	159.20	+ .0022	25,252	+ 1173
27	159.90	158.85	159.85	159.53	+ .0021	25,548	+ 1227
28	162.35	159.75	162.10	161.40	+ .0117	25,671	+ 1527
29	162.60	160.75	160.80	161.38	- .0001	26,438	+ 1524
30	161.40	160.55	161.05	161.00	- .0024	25,710	+ 1462
4/ 2	161.85	159.15	160.00	160.33	- .0042	26,697	+ 1350
3	160.40	158.75	160.15	159.77	- .0035	26,574	+ 1257
4	160.60	159.30	159.60	159.83	+ .0004	26,274	+ 1268
5	160.20	156.30	156.45	157.65	- .0136	25,893	+ 916
6	157.50	155.60	157.45	156.85	- .0051	27,344	+ 777
9	158.00	156.40	157.60	157.33	+ .0031	29,128	+ 867
10	158.60	157.25	157.80	157.88	+ .0035	29,861	+ 972
11	158.10	156.30	156.35	156.92	- .0061	29,657	+ 791
12	160.20	155.30	159.70	158.40	+ .0094	29,362	+ 1067
13	160.85	158.15	158.80	159.27	+ .0055	30,337	+ 1234
16	160.50	157.90	160.40	159.60	+ .0021	27,389	+ 1292
17	161.45	159.75	160.30	160.50	+ .0056	27,267	+ 1139
18	160.30	158.50	159.10	159.30	- .0075	27,640	+ 932
19	159.85	158.40	159.20	159.15	- .0009	27,779	+ 907

81

Chapter 8

Do's And Don'ts In Trading

What you have learned to this point in time is a trading methodology based on the two strongest emotions in humans, i.e., fear and greed. Knowing the trading methodology is not enough. You must also follow a number of trading Do's and Don'ts—trading tactics.

The Do's and Don'ts fall into two areas, general suggestions and tactics and specific rules.

GENERAL SUGGESTIONS

1. *Check The Open Interest Before Putting On A Trade.* Open Interest is the sum total of all the longs and all the shorts in a particular month. Of great importance is what the OI denotes. In one word, liquidity. The higher the OI, the easier it is to put on or take off a position. If the OI is less than 2500, do not put on a position. If the liquidity isn't there, neither are you!

2. *Do Not Anticipate A Trade.* Wait until you have a PI signal. If there is no signal you stay out of the market. Some of the biggest losses to traders are due to their propensity to "jump-the-gun." I cannot stress too strongly this "no-no." Don't trade on hope, because fear will overtake hope.

83

3. *Remove A Portion Of Realized Profits From Time To Time.* Money loses its importance when looked at as a cold figure. Therefore, every so often take out and use some of the profits. You will reaffirm to yourself its importance. Hopefully, this will lead to a greater discipline in your trading.

4. *Record All Conversations Between You And Your AE.* Do this whether you are using a discount futures brokerage firm or a full service company. A recording will protect you in the event the AE makes errors in executing your orders, instructions, etc.

5. *Don't Trade For The Sake Of Trading.* Speculation is a business. To profit, a degree of patience is required. When there is no PI signal, there is no trade.

TRADING SUGGESTIONS AND SPECIFIC RULES

Trendline Trading

1. Upon a penetration of a downsloping line, all short positions should be offset and long positions entered. The stop should be just beneath the PI low preceding the upside break when a new long position is taken.

2. Once a long position is on the books, a second alternative stop may be employed. As the new trendline is drawn in, a second stop can be based on a violation of the trendline.

3. I suggest that your stop strategy be decided based on whether the last PI low is closer to present PI action or whether the trendline butts up against the latest PI movement. Quite often the same stop will take into consideration both the proximity of the PI low and the trendline. The rule: work with the closer stop from either the trendline or PI low. You want to protect accrued profits.

4. Upon a penetration of an upsloping trendline, all long positions should be offset and short positions entered. The stop

should rest just above the PI high preceding the downside break if new short positions are taken. In addition, see rules 1 & 2. The rules are applied the same way, just in the opposite direction.

TRENDLINE FAKEOUT

You've taken a position in a contract based on either a trendline penetration, a PI signal, or both. Within a few days a stop is violated and you are compelled to exit the trade. A week later, the PI reverts and begins moving in the direction of your trade of a week before. You are now in the position of deciding what action to take.

Before addressing the question of whether or not to go back into the original position, let's look at what transpired and your attitude. False breakouts *will* happen. This is part of trading. Learn to accept this truth.

Some traders take the position "once burned, twice shy!" They will not go back into a recent trade which they were faked out of. I, on the other hand, will put on a new position. The market is my road map. If it detoured me out of a previous trade, and is now telling me to go back in, back in I go. It's a new game. This time I hope to win. You ought to consider this point of view in your trading activities. The market is not going to hold a grudge—why should you?

THE DEMISE OF A TRENDLINE

There are times when, after putting on a trade, you sit with it while it procrastinates. You go in on a line break and/or a PI signal. For a couple of days the trade is working. Now, nothing. A meandering, (backing & filling) takes place. A sideways action occurs. This action, too, will befall you.

A trendline rarely moves straight up or down for more than 4 to 6 days. At that time it may lose its strength. A ledge, or sideways PI action takes place. The trendline will cease as it hits the first high or low prior to a sideways action. A trendline connects higher lows or lower tops, not sideways trading.

A new trendline should be started when the PI breaks above or below its recent action.

TRADING TACTICS
FOR A DEAD TRENDLINE

A. if you are not in a trade during a sideways action, stay out of the market until a new trend manifests itself.

B. If you are long or short prior to the sideways trading, stay in the trade until a breakout occurs. If the breakout is against your position, offset the next day. If it's in the same direction in which you have a position, watch the new trendline and/or PI for a signal to get out sometime in the future.

A sideways action may last (unthinkable, but possible) until expiration of the commodity. Don't wait until the last trading month to offset. Close out the trade no later than the last trading day prior to the month in which the contract will expire.

DUPLICITY OF STOPS
—USING THE PI

I mentioned that a stop can be used within the framework of a trendline. Here is how it's found. Assume the PI is moving in staircase fashion, i.e., rises then traces a level (stair) for a few days at which time it moves up again. You can use the preceding PI level as a stop point.

That, coupled (when appropriate or at your discretion) with a violation of a trendline, is a powerful protective profit tactic, indeed. And, too, within a few days (five at most) of one violation in the PI or trendline, a second, confirming signal to offset from the other indicator (PI or trendline) probably will occur.

Chapter 9

Individual Commodities And The PI

OCTOBER 1984 WORLD SUGAR

The Power Index graphs and work forms related to this contract (Figures 21 and 22) will be found on pages 91, 92 and 93. There are two sugar contracts listed for trading, World Sugar and Domestic Sugar. The difference between these contracts is that World Sugar is not subsidized by the U.S. government. Domestic Sugar is subsidized and the price is fixed. Therefore, our work will only consider the World Sugar contract and its options.

The Power Index work form is for the same time period as that used for the June 84 S&P 500 index. This time I have left off the Date and % Change columns. Only the starting and ending date are indicated. I want you to see an abbreviated form without the non-critical data. If you wish, you can insert the weekly dates at the bottom of the PI graph.

While you are gathering data you may occasionally find that today's Average Price is the same as the day before. When this occurs, there will be no adjustment to the open interest, so just drop down the Adjusted OI figure from yesterday into today's slot. Never leave any blanks in your work form, never skip a day on either the form or the graph.

Notice how the trendline on the Average Price section from Day 32 to Day 60 takes on a more severe slope (angle). The slope is quite significant in that it highlights, at times, unmitigated upward and downward pressure on the Average Price. As you draw in the top-to-top or bottom-to-bottom trendlines, fix firmly in your mind the angle of ascent or descent for that contract. They will repeat and your analysis will be more effective when you learn to recognize the usual slopes of the contract's price.

The bottom trendline, when violated, portends much lower prices to come.

The Power Index is scaled at 50 per line. While the numbers look small, you will have no trouble when you actually work with these PI graphs. Remember, too, that when you put a dot indicating the PI value, you will have to approximate where the dot goes between the horizontal lines. An approximation will suffice, so don't worry about pin-point accuracy.

Notice Points 1 and 2 on the PI. The second top (#2) is lower than Top #1. Same as on the Average Price graph. This pattern is a confirmation of a failure in the contract's prices. Lower prices are strongly indicated.

You could have gone short around 8.00. About 4 weeks later, this contract hit a low of 7.17 (closing price, and the low at 4/19/84). A profit of 83 points, at $11.20 per point, would have resulted in a profit of $929.60, and based on the work to date, lower prices are expected, thus larger profits are still hoped for.

Assuming you went short, *where* would you have a mental stop? A couple of points above the first high, of course. The mental stop would be at 8.28, or 28 points ($313.60) above your purchase price. The reason you put the stop above the first high is because the second high did not surpass it, so lower prices were definitely to be expected. In the event there was a reversal, in either the PI or AP, it would mean that higher prices are in store. The high price would touch off the mental stop and you would be out of the position the next day.

FIGURE 21
OCT 84 WORLD SUGAR (CSCE) OPTIONS

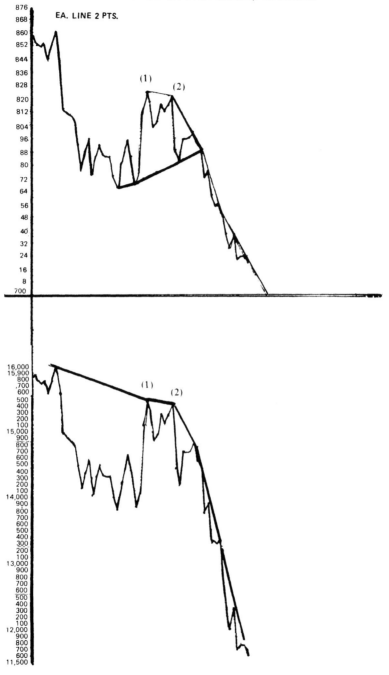

91

FIGURE 22
OCT 1984 WORLD SUGAR (CSCE)

START 1/26/84 - - END 4/19/84

HIGH	LOW	CLOSE	AVG.PR.	OPEN INT.	ADJ. OI
865	844	864	858	15,855	15,855
870	843	846	853	16,065	15,763
860	834	860	851	16,357	15,725
861	845	853	853	17,032	15,765
852	839	841	844	17,325	15,582
856	848	855	853	17,533	15,769
866	858	859	861	17,233	15,932
853	837	839	843	17,322	15,570
822	809	810	814	17,435	14,970
822	800	810	811	17,676	14,905
820	803	807	810	18,030	14,883
812	804	805	807	18,410	14,815
805	785	786	792	18,415	14,473
780	775	779	778	18,588	14,144
795	776	793	788	18,848	14,386
802	790	796	796	19,194	14,581
793	764	766	774	19,343	14,046
790	775	790	785	19,505	14,323
800	781	796	792	19,814	14,500
797	780	781	786	19,988	14,349
789	779	787	785	20,037	14,324
788	782	784	785	20,462	14,324
782	766	770	773	21,020	14,003
770	760	769	766	21,449	13,809
784	775	783	781	21,928	14,238
790	785	788	788	22,243	14,437
797	792	796	795	22,152	14,634
795	778	781	785	22,255	14,354
774	764	766	768	22,450	13,868
780	768	778	775	22,441	14,073
828	778	828	811	22,338	15,111
840	815	818	824	22,091	15,465
827	805	822	818	22,020	15,305
831	782	796	803	22,234	14,897
822	793	799	805	22,362	14,953
832	802	814	816	22,552	15,261
822	803	810	812	23,392	15,146
824	810	814	816	24,283	15,266

FIGURE 22 (CONT'D)
OCT 1984 WORLD SUGAR (CSCE)

START 1/26/84 -- END 4/19/84

HIGH	LOW	CLOSE	AVG.PR.	OPEN INT.	ADJ. OI
830	816	818	821	25,067	15,420
816	770	781	789	25,646	14,420
792	765	788	782	26,390	14,192
800	784	800	796	26,390	14,664
803	780	780	796	26,540	14,664
810	777	804	797	26,744	14,698
806	791	804	800	28,058	14,803
803	787	790	793	28,550	14,553
800	785	786	790	29,775	14,440
785	765	766	772	29,914	13,758
783	765	781	776	30,126	13,914
779	751	753	761	30,085	13,332
764	745	754	754	30,711	13,050
762	751	752	755	31,214	13,092
752	745	747	748	31,213	12,803
750	730	730	737	31,478	12,340
736	723	727	729	30,990	12,004
742	732	736	737	30,549	12,339
735	715	717	722	30,911	11,710
734	711	726	724	31,016	11,796
729	715	728	724	31,023	11,796
728	715	717	720	31,242	11,623

JUNE 1984 D-MARK

The D-Mark, Swiss Franc, Sugar and other futures contracts exhibit in their PI graphs a striking similarity. That is a very good indication. Whether it is a trader in New York buying a D-Mark contract, a trader in Bonn, West Germany purchasing a sugar contract, or a banker in Los Angeles taking a T-Bond position, they all share and express the same emotions. It is those emotions which the Power Index measures.

Traders (investors) respond in much the same manner wherever they live. Year in, year out their emotions, as they apply to trading, do not change. It can be said, with much assurance, that the human animal is a creature of habit and responds through built-in emotions.

If emotions do not change except in intensity, then the ability to measure these emotions will be reflected in similar fashion. That's the reason behind the similarity of individual graphs of the PI showing much the same results. That is also why the PI is so effective in pinpointing the minor to major changes in the evaluation of fear in traders around the world. Always remember, no matter what is being traded or who is doing the trading, fear does not change, only its intensity—and that is what the PI will measure.

At this point, you know how to find the Average Price and Power Index values on a daily basis, and you know that the PI measures the emotion of Fear. You have come a long way. Now, I want to talk to you about two traits which you will have to bring along as you trade the futures markets: patience and discipline.

Referring to the Power Index graphs and work forms (Figures 23 and 24) on pages 97 through 99, notice that between day 2 and day 10 on the work form, the PI difference amounted to a change of 80. Day 2 showed 2612 and day 7, 2692. Subsequent PI readings are much higher. I want to discuss a futures trader's possible reaction during that time period.

There will be spells in which little is going on in the futures contract in which you have, or are contemplating taking, a

94

position. Though it may be frustrating, you must have the patience to wait out the situation until it is time to put on a position. If you do not get a PI signal to take a position in this contract before its life is over, there will be another contract born to take its place. Wait for the PI signal!

On the assumption you already are in a trade, you will have to condition your mind to wait out a do-nothing time frame. To act impulsively is to defeat your reason for putting on the trade in the first place. Discipline will have to be imposed. I can assure you, the movement will get under way before you need to be concerned about expiration.

Looking at the PI graph for the D-Mark, there are a few things I would like to point out. First, notice how I configured the AP section to fit the whole Average Price range. Since you don't start a graph until you have at least 20 days worth of data, you can always make sure you have enough room to encompass the price moves. As long as we are discussing Average Price, I would also like to mention the superiority of using this measure over graphing with single prices, i.e., just the high, or the low, or the close. The Average Price shows the *true* price action. For graphing purposes, it is second to none. The trendline of the Average Price (Figure 23, line #3 on page 97) gives us a clear picture of the direction of prices. Using an average price instead of any one indicator gives you a truer picture of price action, because the average will equalize the off-beat numbers and reveal the essential nature of the price action.

Point 1 is the culmination of the up move in the D-Mark's Average Price graph. Point 2 is a rally that failed. The next day the Average Price broke through the trendline to the downside. At that time, you go short. The stop should be 5 to 10 points above the first top—on a closing basis only.

Point 4 was the culmination of a rally that failed, adding further credence that the short position was the way to go. Points 5 and 6 were anemic attempts of small rallies.

I refrained from drawing in a trendline (downsloping) connecting points 1, 2, 4, and 6, to avoid cluttering up the graph.

But you can see the direction it would take.

The PI mirrored the AP action, with two exceptions. Notice the descending PI line, marked 1 and 1A. It was very (too) sharp in its down move, which was not followed in severity by the drop in the AP. This raised the spectre of a rally in the Average Price, which did, in fact, materialize.

Point 1A to Point 2 on the PI to the upside was not confirmed by the Average Price. As I said before, this non-confirmation to the upside indicates that some tired longs are exiting the market. The down move will commence after this action has abated. As you can see, such results came to pass.

FIGURE 23
JUNE 84 D-MARK OPTIONS (IMM)

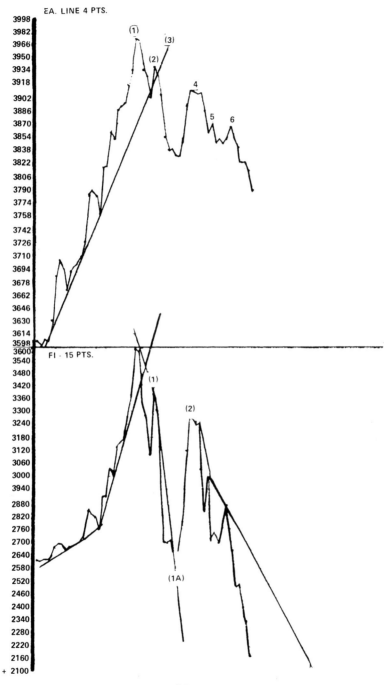

FIGURE 24
JUNE 84 D-MARK (IMM)

Jan.26,'84 - Apr.19,'84

HIGH	LOW	CLOSE	AVG.PR.	OPEN INT.	ADJ. OI
.3616	.3597	.3599	.3604	2,616	2616
.3602	.3594	.3598	.3598	2,627	2612
.3613	.3603	.3604	.3607	2,647	2619
.3608	.3597	.3606	.3604	2,657	2617
.3636	.3620	.3635	.3631	2,850	2638
.3696	.3663	.3695	.3685	2,623	2677
.3720	.3681	.3712	.3704	2,920	2692
.3709	.3683	.3687	.3693	3,337	2682
.3676	.3659	.3666	.3667	3,434	2658
.3699	.3680	.3692	.3690	3,661	2680
.3718	.3678	.3695	.3697	4,021	2687
.3711	.3685	.3701	.3699	4,322	2689
.3713	.3704	.3709	.3709	4,498	2701
.3754	.3688	.3746	.3729	4,911	2736
.3807	.3768	.3778	.3784	7,125	2841
.3803	.3775	.3790	.3789	8,350	2830
.3793	.3774	.3782	.3783	8,994	2816
.3769	.3742	.3768	.3760	9,989	2755
.3842	.3795	.3812	.3817	9,992	2906
.3832	.3798	.3825	.3818	11,711	2909
.3867	.3844	.3862	.3858	11,727	3032
.3862	.3832	.3858	.3851	12,354	3010
.3904	.3872	.3881	.3886	13,739	3135
.3917	.3873	.3882	.3891	14,862	3154
.3905	.3876	.3901	.3894	16,443	3167
.3938	.3901	.3908	.3916	18,935	3274
.3944	.3922	.3937	.3934	21,550	3373
.3985	.3946	.3984	.3972	22,414	3590
.3994	.3950	.3967	.3970	25,749	3577
.3950	.3904	.3947	.3934	26,323	3338
.3940	.3914	.3924	.3926	28,722	3280
.3916	.3883	.3905	.3901	27,303	3106
.3948	.3921	.3945	.3938	29,340	3384
.3954	.3912	.3917	.3928	30,228	3307
.3928	.3885	.3899	.3904	29,928	3124
.3868	.3843	.3847	.3853	32,525	2699
.3861	.3826	.3829	.3839	30,567	2688

FIGURE 24 (CONT'D)
JUNE 84 D-MARK (IMM)

Jan.26,'84 - Apr.19,'84

HIGH	LOW	CLOSE	AVG.PR.	OPEN INT.	ADJ. OI
.3857	.3832	.3835	.3841	29,824	2704
.3847	.3807	.3841	.3832	31,654	2630
.3844	.3822	.3824	.3830	31,051	2614
.3864	.3838	.3855	.3852	30,582	2790
.3903	.3878	.3897	.3893	30,883	3119
.3927	.3900	.3904	.3910	32,660	3262
.3924	.3881	.3923	.3909	32,004	3261
.3925	.3896	.3898	.3906	35,814	3234
.3916	.3890	.3915	.3907	37,878	3244
.3913	.3869	.3871	.3884	36,303	3030
.3880	.3843	.3854	.3859	35,058	2804
.3879	.3852	.3875	.3869	33,700	2891
.3876	.3831	.3837	.3848	33,607	2709
.3862	.3840	.3853	.3852	33,314	2744
.3864	.3834	.3841	.3846	33,686	2692
.3863	.3841	.3857	.3854	33,908	2763
.3878	.3859	.3861	.3866	33,517	2867
.3875	.3837	.3846	.3853	33,931	2753
.3850	.3833	.3843	.3842	33,925	2656
.3835	.3813	.3823	.3824	33,943	2497
.3834	.3812	.3828	.3825	33,648	2506
.3819	.3801	.3819	.3813	34,098	2400
.3811	.3777	.3779	.3789	34,250	2184

DEC 1984 GOLD (CMX)

Every minute of every day (and night) there is an exchange open which trades gold. From Tokyo, to Hong Kong, to Singapore, to London and to the USA, gold is being traded—twenty-four hours a day. What is astounding is, a commodity which trades all over the world, every hour of the day, is still responsive to this technique. The graphs and work forms (Figures 25 and 26) are on pages 101 through 103.

A penetration of a short term Average Price trendline took place at the $411.00 area on day 14. A long position should have been taken between $411.00 and $414.00. On days 30 to 31, you offset when the B-B1 Average Price trendline was violated. The gross profit on the long position ($411.00 to $431.00) was 20 points or $2,000.

A short position at $431.00 and offsetting at Point C, the 60th day on a penetration of a down trendline at a price of $411.00, also would have resulted in a profit of $2,000. Conclusion: Within an eight week period, profits of about $4,000 could have been realized using a long and short strategy.

The Power Index and Average Price mirror each other throughout. The confirmation supports both trading decisions.

A graphing reminder: When I was scaling the Power Index for Gold, I saw that the Adjusted OI numbers, at their widest swing, were about 1500 points apart. Divide this by the 104 lines available to use, and in round numbers, I decided to use 15 points per line.

FIGURE 25
DEC 84 COMEX GOLD (CMX)

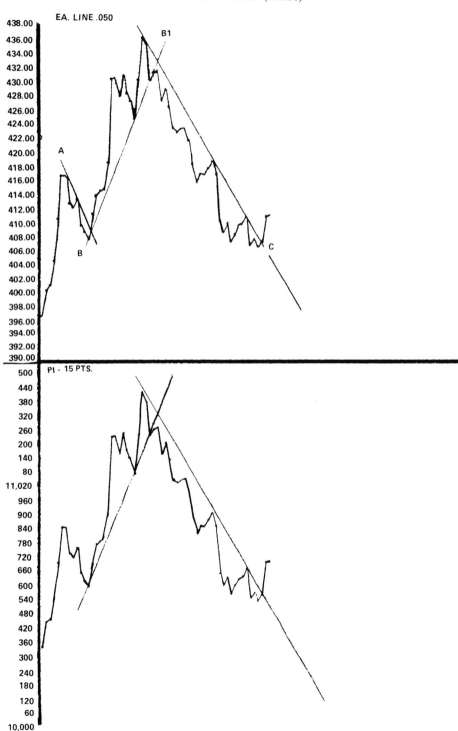

FIGURE 26
DEC 84 COMEX GOLD (CMX)

1-26-84 to 4-19-84

HIGH	LOW	CLOSE	AVG.PR.	OPEN INT.	ADJ. OI
399.20	393.00	397.40	396.53	10,341	10,341
403.00	397.50	400.80	400.43	10,301	10,442
401.50	400.30	401.20	401.00	10,328	10,457
406.00	403.00	404.90	404.63	10,275	10,550
411.50	409.30	411.00	410.60	9,851	10,695
418.50	413.80	418.00	416.77	9,892	10,844
418.50	414.00	417.80	416.77	10,834	10,844
413.50	411.00	413.30	412.60	11,023	10,734
414.00	409.80	412.20	412.00	11,101	10,718
413.70	413.00	413.70	413.46	11,349	10,758
412.00	407.00	409.70	409.57	11,518	10,650
409.50	407.40	408.70	408.53	11,722	10,620
408.50	406.50	407.90	407.63	11,686	10,594
414.10	405.00	414.10	411.07	11,710	10,693
417.00	412.40	412.40	413.93	11,730	10,775
416.00	413.50	414.00	414.50	12,019	10,792
416.00	413.20	415.50	414.90	11,982	10,804
421.50	414.50	419.60	418.53	11,944	10,908
433.50	426.00	431.50	430.33	11,658	11,237
432.50	427.50	431.10	430.37	11,669	11,238
429.50	426.50	427.50	427.83	12,237	11,166
434.00	424.50	433.40	430.63	12,336	11,250
432.50	426.00	426.10	428.20	12,762	11,178
429.20	425.00	426.90	427.03	13,122	11,142
426.50	422.00	425.60	424.70	12,872	11,072
431.60	427.90	431.60	430.37	12,945	11,245
439.00	435.00	435.40	436.47	12,316	11,420
436.20	433.50	435.50	435.07	12,336	11,380
433.50	428.00	429.40	430.30	12,462	11,243
434.00	426.10	433.50	431.20	12,352	11,269
432.50	430.50	431.20	431.40	12,499	11,275
429.00	426.00	426.60	427.20	11,822	11,160
430.50	427.00	428.60	428.70	12,073	11,202
431.00	423.80	423.80	426.20	12,521	11,129
425.50	422.00	422.60	423.37	12,141	11,048

FIGURE 26 (CONT'D)
DEC 84 COMEX GOLD (CMX)

1-26-84 to 4-19-84

HIGH	LOW	CLOSE	AVG.PR.	OPEN INT.	ADJ. OI
424.30	421.30	423.20	422.93	12,118	11,035
424.30	421.50	423.70	423.17	12,360	11,042
423.90	422.00	423.90	423.27	12,508	11,045
422.60	419.50	422.60	421.57	12,631	10,994
422.20	416.00	416.20	418.13	12,551	10,892
418.10	414.00	415.00	415.70	12,524	10,819
418.00	415.50	417.00	416.83	12,638	10,853
418.50	416.00	415.80	416.77	13,278	10,851
420.00	414.00	419.00	417.67	13,317	10,880
419.80	417.50	418.40	418.57	13,350	10,909
418.00	415.70	416.40	416.70	13,361	10,849
416.50	406.50	407.30	410.10	12,885	10,645
409.70	406.70	409.30	408.57	12,775	10,597
410.50	408.80	410.00	409.77	12,443	10,634
410.00	404.50	407.30	407.27	12,376	10,558
409.60	407.00	408.60	408.40	12,476	10,593
410.50	408.60	409.50	409.53	12,468	10,627
411.30	408.30	409.40	409.67	12,475	10,631
412.50	409.70	410.30	410.83	12,929	10,668
410.00	404.30	406.20	406.83	12,920	10,542
408.70	405.30	408.70	407.57	12,376	10,565
407.00	405.70	406.30	406.33	12,565	10,527
408.00	406.50	407.40	407.30	13,251	10,559
415.50	403.50	413.80	410.93	13,463	10,679
412.50	409.50	410.90	410.97	13,687	10,680

DEC 1984 SILVER (COMEX)

Silver is traded in dollars, cents and points. Each 1¢ move is equal to $50.00. Each point move is equal to $0.50. You may see a price of 1054.7 in the paper. Translated, this means $10.5470, or ten dollars, fifty-four and seven-tenths cents (the last zero is usually left off).

Another way the silver price may appear is 1054.0, or ten dollars, fifty-four cents. For our purposes, we will use two places to the right of the decimal point. When you see a price like 1054.0, you will consider it 1054.00; when you see a price like 1054.7, you will consider it 1054.70. Study the Power Index form (Figure 29 on pages 108 and 109) to see how it is written.

Due to the wide fluctuations of silver, I am using two graphs (Figures 27 and 28 on pages 106 and 107), one each for the Power Index and Average Price graphs, for this commodity. Following the procedure used for previous evaluations of price and PI movements, I will use the number of days to indicate salient points. Using two graphs does not detract from your work. Simply place your Average Price graph above your Power Index graph when doing your own price checks.

The scale on the AP graph shows a value of 2¢ per line. The range is between $7.26 and $11.26, or $4.00. Silver can move 50¢ above and below the previous day's closing price. A 1¢ move in silver is equal to $50.00. Is it any wonder, then, that so few traders can profitably trade silver? You need a cast iron stomach to sit through a $2,500 move against your position! Therefore, let the PI be your compass.

The break (Point A, Figure 27 on page 106) of an Average Price trendline should have alerted you to put on a short position. Had you done so at 10.62, within 5 weeks at 9.80, your profit would be $4,100.00. Your first stop would have been at 10.90, equal to .28 or $1,400. The second stop is at 10.50. It was not hit in this time frame.

A beautiful Power Index classic non-confirmation occurred between Points A and A1. The Power Index made a higher high while the Average Price (Point B) failed to confirm.

The Power Index gives you a number of very important signals, which must be recognized. The non-confirmation signal is one. Second is a violation of a Power Index trendline. The longer a Power Index trendline is not violated, the higher the probability of profiting, to the tune of thousands of dollars. Note, too, that when the Power Index line is violated, there is no move back through the trendline. Moral: When the Power Index trendline is finally pierced, you can put on a trade in line with the new direction of the Power Index. A short position is in order when the Power Index is violated to the downside, a long trade if the penetration is to the upside.

FIGURE 27
DEC 84 (COMEX) SILVER (CMX)

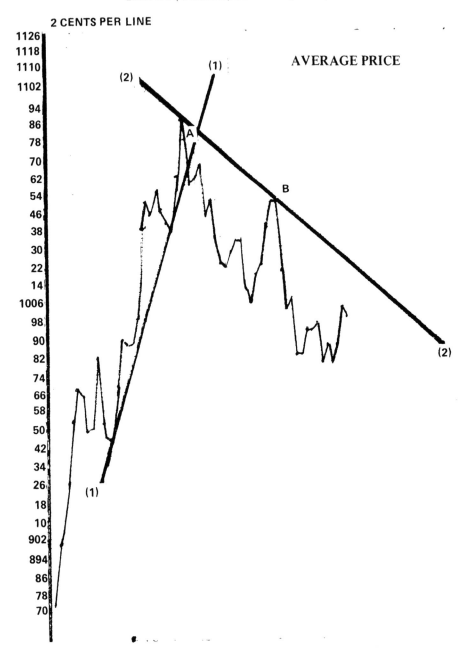

106

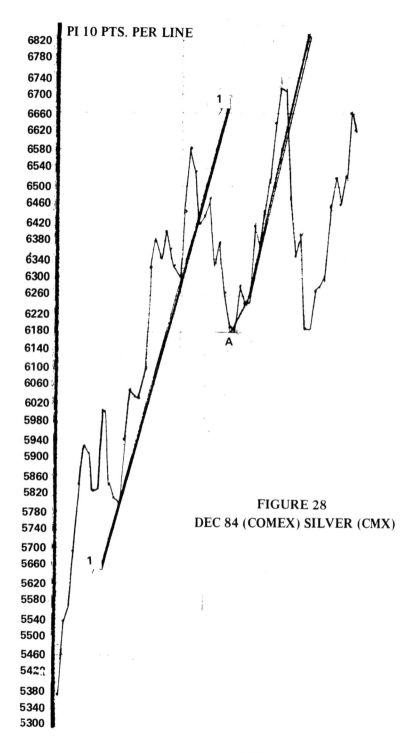

FIGURE 28
DEC 84 (COMEX) SILVER (CMX)

107

FIGURE 29
DEC 84 (COMEX) SILVER (CMX)

Start 1-26-84 To 4-19-84

HIGH	LOW	CLOSE	AVG.PR.	OPEN INT.	ADJ. OI
883.00	857.00	878.50	872.83	5373	5373
910.00	885.00	903.00	899.33	5378	5536
910.00	898.00	907.00	905.00	5338	5570
932.90	913.00	932.90	926.27	5256	5694
960.00	944.00	955.20	953.07	5228	5845
975.00	953.00	971.00	968.00	5238	5927
972.00	953.00	969.90	964.96	5240	5911
956.00	944.00	949.90	949.97	5287	5829
956.00	942.00	953.20	950.40	5300	5831
993.00	979.00	972.50	981.50	5279	6004
980.00	929.00	947.40	952.13	5304	5845
951.00	940.50	947.30	946.27	5313	5812
948.00	942.00	942.30	944.10	5279	5800
988.00	936.00	983.30	969.10	5317	5941
1002.00	981.00	984.30	989.10	5335	6051
998.00	981.70	981.70	987.13	5796	6039
990.40	977.00	990.40	985.93	5419	6032
1008.00	986.00	1000.70	998.23	5359	6099
1050.70	1018.00	1049.70	1039.47	5374	6321
1062.00	1035.00	1055.50	1050.83	5412	6380
1053.00	1039.50	1039.50	1044.00	5469	6344
1073.00	1025.00	1067.70	1055.23	5549	6404
1065.00	1035.00	1041.70	1047.23	5597	6362
1050.00	1030.00	1042.00	1040.67	5739	6326
1043.00	1025.00	1042.00	1036.67	5757	6304
1070.00	1049.00	1067.00	1062.00	5719	6444
1097.00	1081.00	1084.20	1087.40	5827	6583
1085.00	1072.00	1077.60	1078.20	6021	6532
1073.00	1052.00	1052.50	1059.17	6395	6419
1078.00	1033.00	1075.00	1062.00	6564	6437
1080.00	1057.50	1066.00	1067.83	6421	6472
1053.00	1035.00	1044.00	1044.00	6323	6331
1064.00	1040.00	1050.50	1051.50	6476	6378
1065.00	1016.00	1022.00	1034.33	6717	6268
1031.00	1014.00	1022.80	1022.60	6869	6190

FIGURE 29 (CONT'D)
DEC 84 (COMEX) SILVER (CMX)

Start 1-26-84 To 4-19-84

HIGH	LOW	CLOSE	AVG.PR.	OPEN INT.	ADJ. OI
1028.00	1014.00	1021.50	1021.17	6895	6180
1035.00	1018.00	1031.50	1028.17	7007	6228
1038.00	1025.00	1036.20	1033.07	7079	6262
1037.00	1027.00	1035.10	1033.03	7151	6262
1030.00	1000.00	1003.70	1011.23	7200	6414
1016.00	993.00	1006.80	1005.27	7600	6369
1025.00	1007.00	1023.20	1018.40	7618	6468
1030.00	1020.00	1023.60	1024.53	7743	6515
1055.00	1015.00	1052.40	1040.80	7810	6639
1059.00	1046.00	1047.40	1050.80	7845	6714
1056.00	1040.00	1054.10	1050.03	7789	6708
1049.00	1004.10	1004.10	1019.07	8011	6472
1010.50	994.00	1005.10	1003.20	7993	6348
1013.00	1002.00	1006.50	1007.17	7893	6379
1004.00	967.00	977.90	982.97	7895	6189
987.00	977.00	984.90	982.97	8415	6189
998.00	987.00	992.90	992.63	8467	6272
1001.00	985.50	995.00	993.83	8533	6282
1008.00	989.00	993.20	996.73	8651	6307
991.00	968.00	979.30	979.43	8667	6457
994.00	975.00	990.50	986.50	8659	6520
984.00	973.00	982.50	979.83	8782	6461
991.00	981.00	988.50	986.83	8836	6524
1029.00	975.00	1006.00	1003.33	8304	6663
1004.00	994.00	996.70	998.23	8031	6622

DEC 1984 T-BOND (CBT)

Briefly, I want to go over the conversion of a bond or any contract which trades in 32nds. Each 1% move is worth $1,000 so each 32nd is worth $31.25. If we multiply the 32nds by $31.25 and add that to the number of whole points multiplied by $1,000, we come up with the dollar value. So, a price of 66.23 is worth $66,718.75: 23 × 31.25 = 718.75, plus 66 × 1,000 = 66,000.

The numbers to the left of the decimal point are valued in multiples of 1%, or $1,000. The numbers to the right of the decimal are valued in 32nds of a percent, or $31.25 (1000 ÷ 32 = 31.25). The following is a list for converting 32nds.

.01 =	1/32 =	$ 31.25	.17 =	17/32 =	531.25
.02 =	2/32 =	62.50	.18 =	18/32 =	562.50
.03 =	3/32 =	93.75	.19 =	19/32 =	593.75
.04 =	4/32 =	125.00	.20 =	20/32 =	625.00
.05 =	5/32 =	156.25	.21 =	21/32 =	656.25
.06 =	6/32 =	187.50	.22 =	22/32 =	687.50
.07 =	7/32 =	218.75	.23 =	23/32 =	718.75
.08 =	8/32 =	250.00	.24 =	24/32 =	750.00
.09 =	9/32 =	281.25	.25 =	25/32 =	781.25
.10 =	10/32 =	321.50	.26 =	26/32 =	812.50
.11 =	11/32 =	343.75	.27 =	27/32 =	843.75
.12 =	12/32 =	375.00	.28 =	28/32 =	875.00
.13 =	13/32 =	406.25	.29 =	29/32 =	906.25
.14 =	14/32 =	437.50	.30 =	30/32 =	937.50
.15 =	15/32 =	468.75	.31 =	31/32 =	968.75
.16 =	16/32 =	500.00	.00 =	32/32 =	1000.00

The first column is the way the 32nds are expressed in a bond price and is not to be confused with an actual decimal number. Now that you have this list, you can find the dollar equivalent of any quoted bond price just by running down the first column. Please note that 32/32 are never shown, the highest number incorporates the last 32nd. Thus 64.31 is followed by

65.00 as the next highest number.

Two separate graphs will again be used. Since there were large swings in value (Average Price), I did not want to condense the graph by increasing the per line value. Numbered days will again be mentioned to give you a fix on where to look. The Power Index work graphs (Figures 30, 31 and 32) are on pages 112 through 115.

Point A on the Average Price graph (Figure 30, page 112) is where you would have purchased a Dec. contract. Point B is where you would place your initial stop.

Why would you have waited two days after Point B to go into the market at Point A? Look at Points 1 and 2. Both times they were hit, a rally took place, albeit a small one, especially after Point 2. These points now represent a support line. If it was violated, a short position would have been justified, because lower prices are indicated by the violation of previous lows. These lows were eventually broken at B1 -B. You would not have known this until the close, so during the following day (Point A) you went short.

The Power Index (Figure 31 on page 113) showed a steady, unrelenting deterioration. I've drawn in a trendline. If this intermediate line is penetrated to the upside, I would cover the short and go long. A new trend has developed. My stop would have been under the previous low (the low prior to the upside penetration of the trendline).

111

FIGURE 30
DEC 84 T-BONDS (CBT)

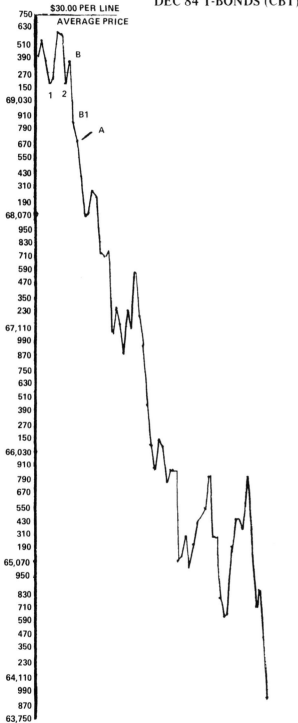

112

FIGURE 31
DEC 84 T-BONDS (CBT)

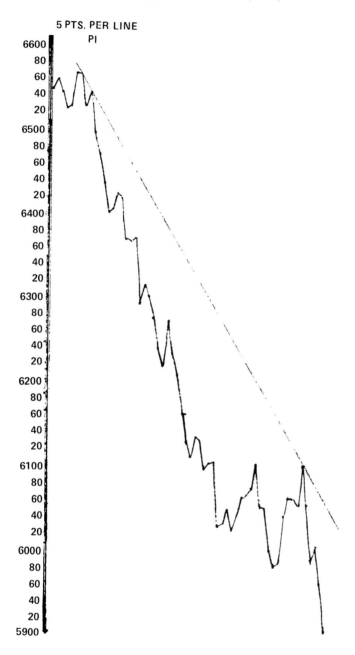

113

FIGURE 32
DEC 84 T-BONDS (CBT)

HIGH	LOW	CLOSE	AVG.PR.	OPEN INT.	ADJ. OI
69,468.75	69,312.50	69,468.75	69,416.67	6548	6548
69,625.00	69,468.75	69,531.25	69,541.67	6527	6559
69,625.00	69,218.75	69,250.00	69,364.58	6475	6543
69,281.25	69,093.75	69,156.25	69,177.08	6488	6525
69,281.25	69,093.75	69,281.25	69,218.75	6693	6529
69,718.75	69,406.25	69,718.75	69,614.58	6661	6567
69,656.25	69,562.50	69,562.50	69,593.75	6561	6565
69,312.50	69,031.25	69,187.50	69,177.08	6406	6527
69,187.50	68,875.00	69,031.25	69,364.58	6451	6544
69,062.50	68,812.50	68,937.50	68,937.50	7681	6497
68,750.00	68,625.00	68,718.75	68,697.92	7450	6471
68,531.25	68,312.50	68,312.50	68,385.42	7457	6437
68,218.75	67,937.50	67,968.75	68,041.67	7323	6400
68,250.00	67,875.00	68,125.00	68,083.33	7322	6404
68,406.25	68,156.25	68,250.00	68,270.83	7359	6424
68,343.75	68,093.75	68,187.50	68,208.33	7235	6417
67,968.75	67,625.00	67,625.00	67,739.58	7200	6368
67,812.50	67,500.00	67,812.50	67,708.33	7204	6365
67,937.50	67,656.25	67,656.25	67,750.00	7770	6370
67,375.00	66,875.00	66,937.50	67,062.50	7691	6292
67,343.75	67,156.25	67,312.50	67,270.83	7120	6314
67,375.00	66,968.75	67,031.25	67,125.00	6872	6299
67,125.00	66,718.75	66,812.50	66,885.42	6952	6274
67,437.50	67,062.50	67,250.00	67,250.00	6635	6238
67,187.50	66,812.50	67,156.25	67,052.08	7252	6217
67,687.50	67,468.75	67,531.25	67,562.50	7015	6270
67,437.50	67,062.50	67,093.75	67,197.92	6950	6232
67,218.75	66,781.25	66,812.50	66,937.50	6741	6206
66,937.50	66,125.00	66,250.00	66,437.50	6029	6161
66,250.00	65,875.00	66,093.75	66,072.92	5974	6128
66,093.75	65,531.25	66,031.25	65,885.42	6103	6111
66,375.00	65,937.50	66,062.50	66,125.00	6175	6133
66,437.50	65,906.25	65,906.25	66,083.33	6129	6129
65,843.75	65,468.75	65,812.50	65,708.33	5944	6095
65,937.50	65,718.75	65,781.25	65,812.50	5941	6104

114

FIGURE 32 (CONT'D)
DEC 84 T-BONDS (CBT)

1-26-84 To 4-19-84

HIGH	LOW	CLOSE	AVG. PR.	OPEN INT.	ADJ. OI
66,343.75	65,531.25	65,531.25	65,802.08	6027	6105
65,343.75	64,875.00	65,000.00	65,072.92	5929	6028
65,343.75	64,781.25	65,218.75	65,114.58	5929	6032
65,500.00	65,125.00	65,218.75	65,281.25	6116	6048
65,156.25	64,781.25	65,156.25	65,031.25	5975	6025
65,468.75	65,062.50	65,125.00	65,218.75	6023	6042
65,531.25	65,312.50	65,406.25	65,416.67	6757	6063
65,781.25	65,281.50	65,312.50	65,458.42	6620	6067
65,687.50	65,218.75	65,687.50	65,531.25	6618	6074
65,906.25	65,625.00	65,875.00	65,802.08	6578	6101
65,531.25	65,156.25	65,156.25	65,281.25	6494	6051
65,593.75	65,093.75	65,125.00	65,270.83	6529	6050
65,031.25	64,531.25	64,750.00	64,770.83	6569	6000
64,875.00	64,406.25	64,531.25	64,604.17	6567	5983
64,843.75	64,468.75	64,625.00	64,645.83	6349	5987
65,312.50	65,031.25	65,281.25	65,208.33	6128	6040
65,593.75	65,156.25	65,562.50	65,437.50	6276	6062
65,687.50	65,312.50	65,312.50	65,437.50	6410	6062
65,437.50	65,218.75	65,406.25	65,354.17	6276	6054
65,875.00	65,687.50	65,875.00	65,812.50	6205	6098
65,968.75	65,000.00	65,062.50	65,343.75	6322	6053
64,906.25	64,500.00	64,656.25	64,687.50	6368	5989
64,906.25	64,718.75	64,906.25	64,843.75	7125	6006
64,843.75	64,218.75	64,218.75	64,427.08	7191	5960
64,093.75	63,750.00	63,937.50	63,927.08	7237	5904

JULY 1984 WHEAT

Basically, there is no difference between grain and other contracts. However, since you will be working with fractions, you will have to know how to convert them to whole numbers in order to obtain the Average Price. Secondly, since the Average Price can be any whole number and remainder, you will have to bring that figure to the nearest grain price. Really no problem.

Assume the high, low and closing prices of the July (CBT) Wheat contract are 348, 343¾, and 345¼. First change the fractions to whole numbers: 348 becomes 348.00, 343¾ becomes 343.75 and 345¼ becomes 345.25.

Adding the three prices together and dividing by 3, we get an Average Price of 345.67, rounded off. Since there are only four ways to write out a grain price, .25, .50, .75, and .00, we have to alter the average price slightly. Keep in mind this procedure is used only for graphing. Since .67 is closest to .75, we will use an average price of 345.75. If the calculation produced an Average Price of 345.62, we would have used 345.50, as this is the closest grain price. This method only applies to grains and only for graphing purposes. We use the Average Price, without the alteration, for % Change calculations.

The related Power Index graphs and forms for the Wheat contract (Figures 33 and 34) are located on pages 118 through 120. Go long about $236.00 on the breakout to the upside (Point A). When offset at Point C, this would have resulted in a profit of 24¢, or $1,200.00 in six weeks. The stop is at $323.00, or a risk of only $150.00.

A short position should have been put on at the time the long position was offset. The initial stop is at $359.00, about 9¢ away from the entry point. In terms of dollars, a $450 stop loss.

On April 26th, 1984 (not shown), four business days from where I stopped, the low for July Wheat was 343.75, and the close was 345.25. An accrued profit on the short side of .0475 cents or $237.50.

Note the sharp difference in the angle between Point A and

Points B and C. Any time you notice such a deviation up or · down (see line 1 - 1A), a reversal in direction is close at hand. Something to keep in the back of your mind. Let us now look at the Power Index and the message it was sending to us.

The A1 - A2 trendline's angle became acute. A breakout to the upside was close at hand. The signal to go long was registered a few days before it became evident on the price graph (see the arrow at A2).

The trendline B, C, and D, indicates how it is turning to the right at sharper and sharper (more acute) angles of ascent. The angle at E shows a curling over. A penetration which occurred (not shown) gave a signal that the upmove in the July Wheat contract was at an end. When line D was violated, the long position should have been offset and a short position taken.

When you see a PI and AP signal to offset your position, do it. Then, and only then, consider a trade in the opposite direction.

At the beginning of this book, I told you that you would be taught how to trade futures contracts one way. My reasoning was based on the idea, "If it works, don't fix it!" Stay away from altering your trading strategy if you want to make money in futures trading.

COCOA

This contract trades in metric tons. The prices are in thousands of dollars for the whole contract. A price of 2.577 for cocoa means $2,557.00. Use the whole number as thousands of dollars in your work.

SOYMEAL

To find the price of meal, which is traded in 100 tons, simply change the price to thousands of dollars rather than hundreds of dollars, as shown in the newspaper. For example, a price of 186.10 becomes $18,610.00. Now, all you need do is enter the prices on the Power Index form and begin the procedure to obtain the Average Price.

FIGURE 33
JULY 84 WHEAT (CBT)

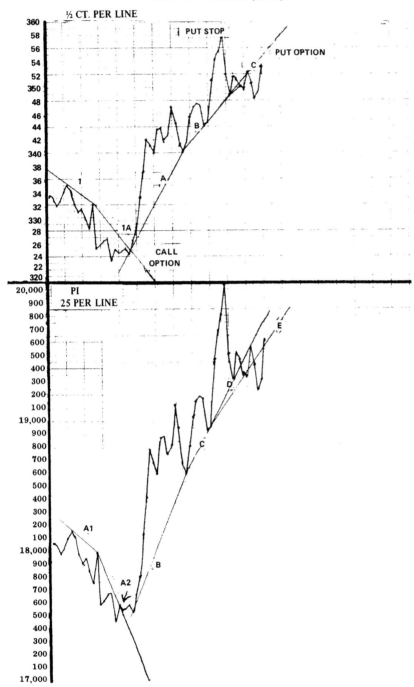

118

FIGURE 34
JULY 84 WHEAT (CBT)

1-26-84 To 4-19-84

HIGH	LOW	CLOSE	AVG.PR.	OPEN INT.	ADJ. OI
336.50	331.00	332.50	333.33	18,039	18,039
336.50	331.00	331.25	332.92	17,359	18,018
333.00	329.25	332.75	331.67	18,048	17,951
333.50	331.25	332.50	332.42	17,795	17,991
335.00	332.00	335.00	334.00	18,095	18,077
336.50	333.50	335.00	335.00	18,114	18,131
335.00	333.00	334.25	334.08	18,613	18,080
333.75	330.50	331.50	331.92	18,814	17,958
332.00	330.00	330.25	330.75	19,076	17,891
333.00	329.50	331.50	331.33	19,199	17,925
331.00	328.50	329.50	329.67	18,331	17,828
330.00	327.00	327.50	328.17	19,444	17,740
343.50	326.00	326.50	332.00	19,446	17,967
327.75	323.75	324.25	325.25	19,228	17,576
326.25	325.00	326.00	325.75	19,343	17,606
327.25	325.50	327.00	326.58	19,650	17,656
328.50	325.00	326.50	326.67	19,833	17,661
325.00	322.00	322.50	323.17	19,819	17,449
327.00	323.00	325.25	325.08	20,325	17,569
326.25	322.75	324.75	324.58	20,896	17,537
325.75	323.25	325.25	324.75	20,991	17,548
326.25	323.25	326.00	325.17	21,110	17,575
327.00	322.50	323.25	324.25	21,525	17,514
329.00	322.50	327.75	326.42	21,398	17,657
330.00	325.50	329.50	328.33	21,716	17,784
334.00	331.00	334.00	333.00	22,711	18,107
339.00	333.50	338.75	337.08	22,791	18,386
345.25	338.00	343.75	342.33	22,992	18,744
342.00	338.50	342.00	340.83	23,813	18,640
341.00	337.25	341.00	339.75	24,645	18,562
345.00	340.25	345.00	343.42	24,376	18,825
345.75	341.50	342.00	343.67	24,886	18,843
343.75	340.50	341.25	341.83	24,625	18,711
344.00	340.50	343.75	342.75	24,888	18,778

FIGURE 34 (CONT'D)
JULY 84 WHEAT (CBT)

1-26-84 To 4-19-84

HIGH	LOW	CLOSE	AVG.PR.	OPEN INT.	ADJ. OI
348.50	344.25	347.75	346.83	25,041	19,076
348.00	342.00	343.50	344.50	25,425	18,905
342.50	339.25	341.00	340.92	25,484	18,640
342.50	336.75	340.75	340.00	25,314	18,573
344.50	340.25	342.75	342.50	26,163	18,765
349.50	340.50	346.25	345.42	26,371	18,990
347.50	346.00	347.50	347.00	26,630	19,112
348.50	346.50	347.25	347.42	26,462	19,144
351.00	345.25	345.25	347.17	26,668	19,125
346.25	342.50	344.00	344.25	27,577	18,893
345.75	343.25	344.75	344.58	27,482	18,919
355.00	343.50	354.50	351.00	27,125	19,424
357.50	351.00	353.00	353.83	26,789	19,640
357.50	352.25	356.25	355.33	27,419	19,756
360.00	357.75	357.25	358.33	28,160	19,994
354.75	350.00	350.25	351.67	28,645	19,462
351.00	347.00	348.25	348.75	28,546	19,225
352.75	350.00	352.00	351.58	28,765	19,458
352.50	348.50	352.25	351.08	28,624	19,417
352.75	348.00	349.00	349.92	28,686	19,322
351.75	346.50	350.25	349.50	28,683	19,288
354.00	349.50	353.00	352.17	27,903	19,501
353.50	348.50	349.75	350.58	27,954	19,375
350.75	346.75	347.00	348.17	27,440	19,186
351.75	345.00	350.75	349.17	27,610	19,265
354.75	350.00	354.25	353.00	27,409	19,566

JULY 1984 SOYBEANS

The Power Index construction, as well as the procedure for obtaining the Average Price, on Soybeans is exactly the same as for Wheat. Therefore, we will skip the preliminaries. The time frame studied is from January 26 to April 19, 1984, inclusive. The Power Index graphs and work forms (Figures 35 and 36) are on pages 123 to 125.

Analyzing the Average Price, we see Line A denotes a downtrend in Beans, which came to an end on Day 15. On the following day (Day 16), at a price of $7.36, a long position should have been taken.

The long position would have been offset on Day 35, between $7.94 and $8.01. On Day 34, the B line was penetrated. You would not have known until after the market closed. That is why I am using the next trading day to offset the long position (see arrow). A profit, using the low for Day 35 ($7.91), would have been, at the minimum, $2,750.00—in just 19 days!

The C trendline illuminated, in crystal clarity, the need to pay attention to the slope (angle) of the trendline as it becomes more extreme. The angle, beginning at C1 and going to C2, is about 82°. The angle from C to C1 is approximately 40°! You do not have to measure the angles, a visual inspection is all you need do. Just be alert to a sharper line, up or down, than previously evidenced. This will alert you to the probable near term reversal of the existing trend.

At C2, on the 51st day, a short signal in the contract was evident when the Average Price penetrated the C2 trendline. This occurred on Day 50. Go short at $8.00. Eight days later, Beans were at $7.80.

Notice Points 1 and 2 (Days 55 and 57, respectively). The price tested the $7.80 level twice and bounced off. Obviously, since Beans did not violate the support to the downside, they were going higher near term.

A stop should have been placed (mental) at the $7.86 level.

The reason being that if Beans were in fact reversing to the upside, this price was far enough away to confirm a new uptrend if the stop was hit. The profit is about $700.00.

While the Power Index matched the Average Price with respect to long and short signals, I want to draw your attention to Line D - D1 on this index. The upside breakout was your signal to offset the short position. When in doubt, always refer to the Power Index to find the answer. The crucial part of a system is to always stick to the rules and use the tools you have available.

FIGURE 35
JULY 84 SOYBEANS

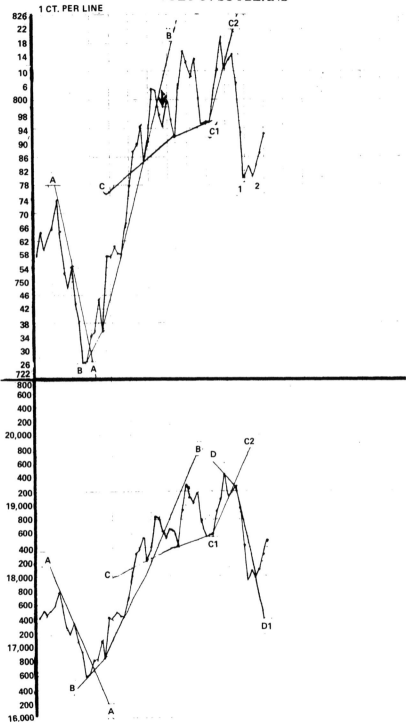

FIGURE 36
JULY 84 SOYBEANS

1-26-84 To 4-19-84

HIGH	LOW	CLOSE	AVG.PR.	OPEN INT.	ADJ. OI
768.00	751.50	753.25	757.58	17,405	17,405
771.00	761.00	761.50	764.50	17,350	17,563
764.00	751.50	762.75	759.42	17,621	17,445
767.50	759.50	760.50	762.50	17,435	17,516
770.00	758.00	768.00	765.33	17,799	17,582
777.50	771.00	772.75	773.75	18,334	17,784
768.00	762.50	764.00	764.83	18,376	17,572
760.50	740.50	755.50	752.17	18,420	17,267
756.50	740.00	750.25	748.92	18,614	17,187
760.00	748.50	755.75	754.75	18,671	17,332
756.00	737.50	738.25	743.92	19,142	17,057
744.50	734.25	737.00	738.58	19,603	16,916
733.00	720.50	725.75	726.42	19,558	16,594
736.00	720.00	725.50	727.17	19,334	16,614
738.00	728.50	736.25	734.25	19,339	16,802
740.00	733.00	734.25	735.75	19,051	16,841
750.50	738.00	745.25	744.58	19,218	17,072
741.50	728.50	737.50	735.83	18,999	16,849
767.50	746.00	759.50	757.67	19,095	17,416
762.50	752.00	756.50	757.00	20,284	17,398
764.00	756.00	760.75	760.25	20,397	17,486
762.00	752.00	761.50	758.50	21,101	17,437
768.50	752.00	753.50	758.00	22,506	17,422
775.50	752.00	773.50	767.00	22,635	17,691
781.50	771.75	778.50	777.25	23,209	18,001
793.00	782.50	786.50	787.33	23,547	18,306
796.50	777.50	795.50	789.83	24,821	18,385
800.00	789.50	793.50	794.33	25,589	18,531
788.00	780.00	787.50	785.17	25,940	18,232
796.50	779.50	795.75	790.58	25,841	18,410
808.00	795.00	807.00	803.33	26,296	18,834
808.50	799.00	799.50	802.33	27,013	18,800
806.00	793.00	793.50	797.50	27,466	18,635
798.50	788.50	796.00	794.33	27,539	18,526
805.50	794.00	804.50	801.33	28,016	18,773

FIGURE 36 (CONT'D)
JULY 84 SOYBEANS

1-26-84 To 4-19-84

HIGH	LOW	CLOSE	AVG.PR.	OPEN INT.	ADJ. OI
809.50	789.00	791.75	796.75	28,071	18,613
795.00	785.00	794.50	791.50	28,726	18,424
817.00	785.50	816.00	806.17	28,245	18,948
823.00	810.00	813.00	815.33	28,498	19,272
819.00	807.00	810.00	812.00	29,581	19,151
816.00	801.00	808.50	808.50	30,049	19,021
817.00	810.00	812.50	813.17	29,944	19,194
814.00	796.00	796.50	802.17	29,619	18,793
800.00	790.50	795.75	795.42	28,609	18,552
802.00	792.00	793.50	795.83	28,890	18,567
800.00	788.50	799.25	795.92	29,036	18,570
814.50	795.50	805.25	805.08	28,815	18,902
814.00	803.00	813.50	810.17	29,263	19,087
823.00	816.00	820.00	819.67	29,597	19,434
816.50	806.50	808.75	810.58	29,616	19,106
817.00	806.50	815.75	813.08	29,492	19,197
821.50	811.00	812.00	814.83	29,772	19,261
810.50	804.00	805.00	806.50	30,066	18,954
808.00	784.00	785.00	792.33	30,432	18,419
784.50	775.50	780.00	780.00	30,968	17,945
787.00	779.00	783.25	783.08	30,322	18,066
784.50	775.50	781.75	780.58	30,514	17,969
787.50	781.50	782.25	783.75	31,508	18,097
794.00	775.00	792.50	787.17	33,194	18,242
796.50	789.00	793.25	792.92	34,543	18,494

125

DECEMBER 1984 EURODOLLAR

So called savvy corporations have been getting killed due to the movement of American interest rate fluctuations vis a vis European interest rate movements; specifically, Eurodollar rates. While it is not within the scope of this work to offer these firms hedging strategies, it is worth noting the problems they have. We will be studying the Dec 1984 Eurodollar contract with an eye toward trading it the way it should be traded, using the Power Index.

The Power Index graphs and work forms (Figures 37 and 38) are on pages 127 through 129.

Line A, 28th day. A PI breakthrough started. A short position was initiated on Day 29, at a price of 88.46. The Power Index did not give a reversal from that time. Notice that the Line B trendline was never violated to the upside. The Average price on Day 60 was 87.59. To this point in time, the short had an accrued profit of 87 points. At $25 a point, a profit of $2,175 could have been taken in just 21 days!

The downsloping trendline drawn in on the Average Price graph mirrors the action of the Power Index line (line B) which depicts the fear exacerbation of the traders.

FIGURE 37
DEC 84 EURODOLLARS

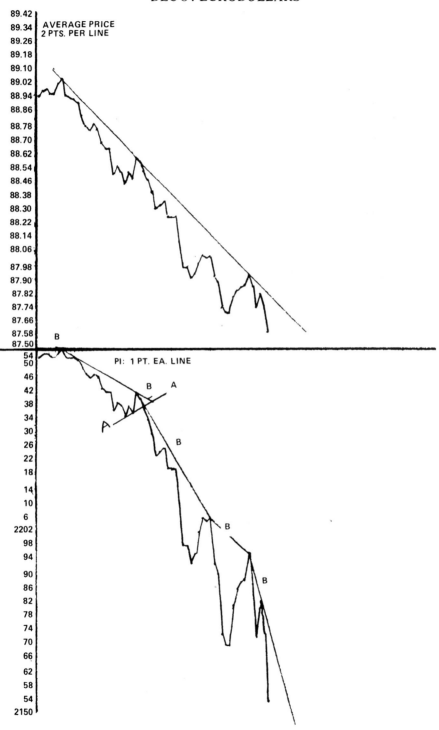

127

FIGURE 38
DEC 84 EURODOLLAR

1-26-84 To 4-19-84

HIGH	LOW	CLOSE	AVG.PR.	OPEN INT.	ADJ. OI
88.96	88.92	88.93	88.94	2251	2251
88.98	88.96	88.96	88.97	2265	2252
89.02	88.96	88.96	88.98	2360	2252
88.97	88.93	88.94	88.95	2535	2251
88.96	88.93	88.95	88.95	2581	2251
89.04	88.98	89.01	89.01	2597	2253
89.06	89.03	89.03	89.04	2722	2254
88.97	88.91	88.94	88.94	2829	2251
88.94	88.91	88.93	88.93	2923	2251
88.93	88.90	88.93	88.92	3049	2251
88.91	88.88	88.91	88.90	3030	2250
88.88	88.80	88.81	88.83	3091	2248
88.80	88.76	88.76	88.77	3108	2246
88.76	88.72	88.76	88.75	3145	2245
88.81	88.75	88.77	88.78	3212	2246
88.78	88.74	88.74	88.75	3266	2245
88.70	88.65	88.65	88.67	3367	2242
88.65	88.62	88.64	88.64	3455	2241
88.69	88.61	88.61	88.64	3469	2241
88.58	88.46	88.46	88.50	3447	2236
88.56	88.51	88.56	88.54	3642	2238
88.61	88.46	88.46	88.51	3629	2237
88.47	88.42	88.44	88.44	4144	2234
88.53	88.49	88.50	88.51	4365	2237
88.48	88.45	88.48	88.47	4471	2235
88.60	88.56	88.60	88.59	4620	2241
88.64	88.52	88.52	88.56	4797	2239
88.54	88.49	88.50	88.51	4800	2236
88.55	88.41	88.42	88.46	4909	2233
88.42	88.37	88.38	88.39	5269	2229
88.32	88.25	88.32	88.30	5547	2223
88.35	88.29	88.31	88.32	6005	2224
88.38	88.32	88.32	88.34	6133	2225
88.29	88.21	88.24	88.25	6336	2219
88.27	88.21	88.26	88.25	6494	2219
88.35	88.20	88.20	88.25	6526	2219
88.17	88.07	88.08	88.11	6594	2209
88.08	87.87	87.93	87.96	6946	2197
87.98	87.94	87.95	87.96	7528	2197
87.94	87.85	87.91	87.90	7855	2192

FIGURE 38 (CONT'D)
DEC 84 EURODOLLAR

1-26-84 To 4-19-84

HIGH	LOW	CLOSE	AVG.PR.	OPEN INT.	ADJ. OI
87.98	87.90	87.91	87.93	8,245	2195
88.01	87.97	88.00	87.99	8,462	2201
88.10	87.99	87.99	88.03	8,787	2205
88.04	87.99	88.03	88.02	8,816	2204
88.09	87.99	88.00	88.03	9,171	2205
87.97	87.88	87.88	87.91	9,343	2192
87.97	87.83	87.84	87.88	9,457	2189
87.81	87.67	87.71	87.73	9,874	2172
87.73	87.67	87.70	87.70	10,179	2169
87.78	87.63	87.68	87.70	10,375	2169
87.83	87.74	87.81	87.79	10,473	2180
87.85	87.79	87.85	87.83	10,525	2185
87.88	87.83	87.84	87.85	10,672	2187
87.88	87.84	87.87	87.86	10,643	2188
87.96	87.86	87.95	87.92	10,822	2195
87.97	87.79	87.79	87.85	10,895	2186
87.78	87.68	87.72	87.73	10,876	2171
87.83	87.76	87.83	87.81	10,904	2181
87.79	87.71	87.72	87.74	10,992	2172
87.62	87.56	87.58	87.59	10,967	2153

JUNE 1984 HEATING OIL NO. 2

Admittedly, heating oil is not the best futures contract to trade. During the few months of recorded data used, the contract had a range of 475 points. A point has a value of $4.20. Thus, in terms of dollars, we are looking at a move of $1,995. The Power Index graphs and work forms (Figures 39 and 40) are on pages 131 through 133.

The scale for the Average Price graph is in multiples of 5 points per line. A two point change per line is used for the Power Index.

The Power Index gave a signal to go long based on a trendline penetration on Day 15. On Day 16, a long position was taken at .7455.

Notice that the large move in the price of the contract did not take place until Day 19, giving you a full 3 days to position yourself.

An offsetting signal was triggered on the close of trading on Day 27. Although the price did move slightly higher over the next few days, the PI indicated that the back of the bull move had been broken, to that point in time. Average Price on Day 28 was .7770.

Day 41 presented us with a second signal to go long, which we did on Day 42. The Average Price was .7710. An offsetting signal occurred on Day 50 based on the penetration of a trendline. We offset the next day (51) at an Average Price of .7700. The loss of .10 points amounted to $42.

The profit on the first long trade was 315 points, or $1,323.00, against a loss on the second option trade of $42.00. The net profit, not including commissions, was $1,281.00!

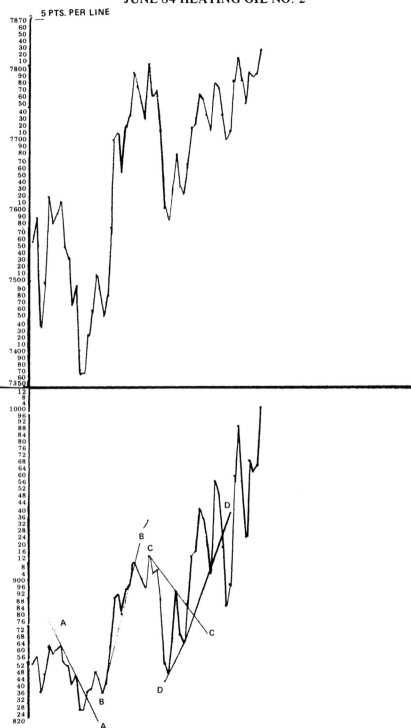

FIGURE 39
JUNE 84 HEATING OIL NO. 2

5 PTS. PER LINE

FIGURE 40
JUNE 84 HEATING OIL NO. 2

Start: 1-26-84 to 4-19-84

HIGH	LOW	CLOSE	AVG.PR.	OPEN INT.	ADJ. OI
.7590	.7525	.7550	.7555	852	852
.7625	.7570	.7570	.7588	929	856
.7510	.7370	.7420	.7433	996	836
.7590	.7400	.7500	.7497	1,005	846
.7625	.7610	.7619	.7618	972	862
.7650	.7550	.7550	.7583	971	858
.7630	.7560	.7600	.7596	1,030	860
.7630	.7580	.7630	.7613	1,064	862
.7610	.7500	.7530	.7547	1,075	853
.7575	.7510	.7512	.7532	1,042	851
.7500	.7440	.7460	.7467	1,108	841
.7520	.7465	.7495	.7493	1,107	845
.7460	.7310	.7327	.7366	1,108	826
.7420	.7270	.7415	.7368	1,320	826
.7475	.7360	.7430	.7422	1,357	836
.7500	.7410	.7460	.7457	1,321	838
.7535	.7480	.7512	.7509	1,470	847
.7610	.7430	.7430	.7490	1,437	843
.7485	.7400	.7460	.7448	1,421	835
.7530	.7375	.7530	.7478	1,444	841
.7630	.7510	.7586	.7575	1,539	861
.7786	.7565	.7750	.7700	1,706	889
.7820	.7650	.7656	.7709	1,874	891
.7683	.7600	.7673	.7652	1,527	880
.7735	.7695	.7720	.7717	1,592	894
.7780	.7670	.7750	.7733	1,595	897
.7815	.7750	.7815	.7793	1,610	909
.7805	.7750	.7765	.7773	1,566	905
.7810	.7715	.7724	.7750	1,687	900
.7750	.7690	.7745	.7728	1,768	895
.7825	.7785	.7805	.7805	1,789	913
.7770	.7745	.7765	.7760	1,820	903
.7800	.7740	.7764	.7768	1,840	905
.7750	.7680	.7703	.7711	2,285	888
.7690	.7630	.7653	.7602	2,595	852
.7640	.7550	.7567	.7586	2,996	846
.7700	.7510	.7675	.7628	3,525	866
.7739	.7645	.7653	.7679	3,979	893
.7700	.7590	.7606	.7632	4,004	868
.7650	.7575	.7643	.7623	3,930	863

FIGURE 40 (CONT'D)
JUNE 84 HEATING OIL NO. 2

Start: 1-26-84 to 4-19-84

HIGH	LOW	CLOSE	AVG.PR.	OPEN INT.	ADJ. OI
.7700	.7645	.7653	.7666	3,992	886
.7745	.7687	.7716	.7716	4,074	913
.7770	.7675	.7722	.7722	4,223	916
.7885	.7700	.7706	.7764	4,432	940
.7780	.7720	.7772	.7757	5,756	935
.7770	.7685	.7751	.7735	5,508	919
.7737	.7670	.7731	.7713	5,700	903
.7800	.7740	.7798	.7779	6,225	956
.7800	.7740	.7770	.7770	6,402	949
.7775	.7695	.7734	.7735	6,786	918
.7725	.7660	.7714	.7700	7,236	885
.7735	.7675	.7729	.7713	7,000	897
.7830	.7720	.7799	.7783	6,851	959
.7850	.7770	.7824	.7815	7,147	988
.7835	.7745	.7765	.7782	7,564	956
.7775	.7705	.7770	.7750	7,732	924
.7825	.7755	.7801	.7794	7,664	968
.7810	.7755	.7798	.7788	7,880	962
.7820	.7760	.7795	.7792	7,995	966
.7840	.7800	.7834	.7825	7,796	999

133

JUNE 1984 CATTLE

The Power Index graphs and work forms (Figures 41 and 42) are on pages 135 through 137.

During the 60 days of recorded action, a futures trader could have taken 5 positions in the June Live Cattle contract.

1. Upon the penetration of Line A, a short position could have been taken, on Day 12.

2. On Day 14, an offsetting Power Index signal was triggered. The short position should have been closed and a long position initiated.

3 On Day 28, the long position was offset and a short position put on.

4. On Day 40, the short position was offset and a long position taken.

5. On Day 51, the long position was offset and a short position taken. The short position was offset on Day 58.

FIGURE 41
JUNE 84 CATTLE

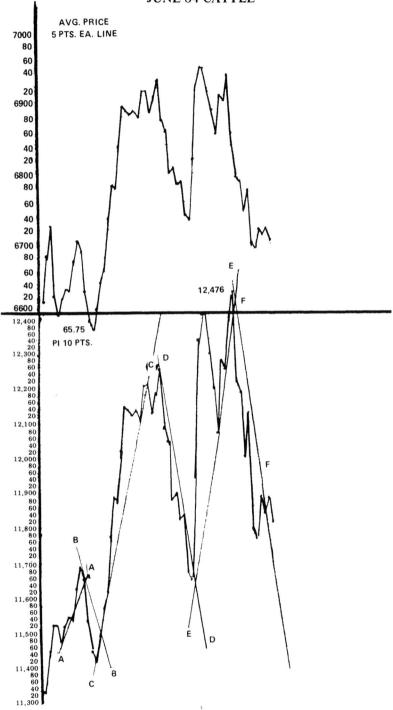

135

FIGURE 42
JUNE 84 CATTLE

1-26-84 To 4-19-84

HIGH	LOW	CLOSE	AVG.PR.	OPEN INT.	ADJ. OI
66.62	65.90	65.95	66.16	11,337	11,337
67.15	66.25	67.05	66.82	11,641	11,453
67.55	66.90	67.27	67.24	11,613	11,526
66.90	65.77	66.05	66.24	11,880	11,526
66.25	65.60	66.10	65.98	12,428	11,478
66.45	65.80	66.35	66.20	12,898	11,521
66.60	65.92	66.50	66.34	13,121	11,549
66.72	66.05	66.17	66.31	13,047	11,543
67.00	66.40	66.85	66.75	13,186	11,630
67.25	66.65	67.22	67.04	13,706	11,690
67.20	66.55	66.90	66.88	13,701	11,657
66.90	65.95	66.02	66.29	13,567	11,537
66.15	65.50	65.95	65.87	13,551	11,451
66.10	65.55	65.60	65.75	13,990	11,426
66.60	65.10	66.52	66.07	14,202	11,495
66.72	66.25	66.32	66.43	14,325	11,573
67.00	65.95	66.97	66.64	14,718	11,620
67.72	66.70	67.62	67.35	14,868	11,778
68.02	67.52	67.95	67.83	15,263	11,887
68.15	67.37	67.82	67.78	15,450	11,876
68.75	67.65	68.70	68.37	15,667	12,012
69.35	68.65	68.80	68.93	16,397	12,146
69.30	68.62	68.72	68.88	17,830	12,133
69.15	68.25	69.10	68.83	17,927	12,120
69.20	68.65	68.82	68.89	18,339	12,136
69.10	68.45	68.82	68.79	18,454	12,109
69.40	68.92	69.12	69.15	18,381	12,205
69.35	68.95	69.20	69.17	18,777	12,210
69.20	68.62	68.77	68.86	19,248	12,124
69.30	68.65	69.27	69.07	19,263	12,183
69.67	69.10	69.15	69.31	19,207	12,250
69.10	68.55	68.60	68.75	19,738	12,091
69.05	68.35	68.37	68.59	19,771	12,045
68.40	67.80	67.85	68.02	20,414	11,875
68.45	67.62	68.10	68.06	20,570	11,887
68.07	67.70	67.77	67.85	21,924	11,824
68.10	67.70	67.87	67.89	22,112	11,837
68.10	67.00	67.07	67.39	22,087	11,674
67.70	67.10	67.20	67.33	22,843	11,654
68.67	67.42	68.52	68.20	23,834	11,962

FIGURE 42 (CONT'D)
JUNE 84 CATTLE

1-26-84 To 4-19-84

HIGH	LOW	CLOSE	AVG.PR.	OPEN INT.	ADJ. OI
69.50	68.75	69.45	69.23	24,683	12,335
69.85	69.25	69.30	69.47	24,291	12,419
69.80	69.27	69.35	69.47	25,447	12,419
69.50	68.87	69.05	69.14	26,003	12,295
69.07	68.70	68.90	68.89	26,145	12,200
68.75	68.20	68.70	68.55	26,100	12,071
69.52	68.40	69.32	69.08	26,312	12,274
69.30	68.80	68.95	69.02	27,349	12,250
69.70	69.20	69.22	69.37	27,886	12,391
69.55	68,05	68.10	68.57	29,415	12,476
68.40	67.70	67.75	67.95	28,961	12,214
68.35	67.52	67.80	67.89	29,050	12,188
67.72	67.10	67.60	67.47	29,825	12,003
67.92	67.45	67.87	67.75	29,281	12,125
67.65	66.57	66.77	67.00	29,780	11,795
67.15	66.62	67.05	66.94	28,624	11,769
67.40	66.87	67.35	67.21	28,862	11,885
67.35	66.97	67.02	67.11	28,679	11,842
67.37	67.05	67.22	67.21	28,387	11,884
67.65	66.62	66.85	67.04	27,944	11,813

OCTOBER 1984 COTTON

Cotton, although listed on the New York Cotton Exchange, is traded by professionals (cotton brokers, growers and users) and the public around the world. This is so because cotton is a "staple" in most economies. What never fails to amuse this writer is how cotton (and other commodities) is responsive to the signals emanating from the Power Index, even though cotton is subject to the political/economic policies of states. This proves, once again, that fear and greed are what moves prices. The Power Index graphs and work forms (Figures 43 and 44) are on pages 139 through 141.

The Power Index signals. At the outset, be aware of the fact that you are not going to get in at the bottom of a move, nor will you exit at the very top of a price run-up. The Power Index signals can and will allow you to capture a very large part of a trend, as follows.

1. The penetration of Line A, which occurred on Day 14, indicated that a long trade should have been put on at .7280 cents on Day 15. Checking the Average Price graph, we find the price was indeed at 72.80, some forty points above its low.

2. On Day 49, the PI suggested that the long position be offset on the following day (50). The Average Price on Day 50 was 77.11.

3. The difference between 77.11 and 72.80 is 431 points. At $5 a point, the profit (not including commissions) is $2,155.

4. This profit took 35 days to develop!

5. The top of the move occurred on Day 48, at an Average Price of 78.70, or 159 points off the high. This is what I mean by taking a major chunk out of a move.

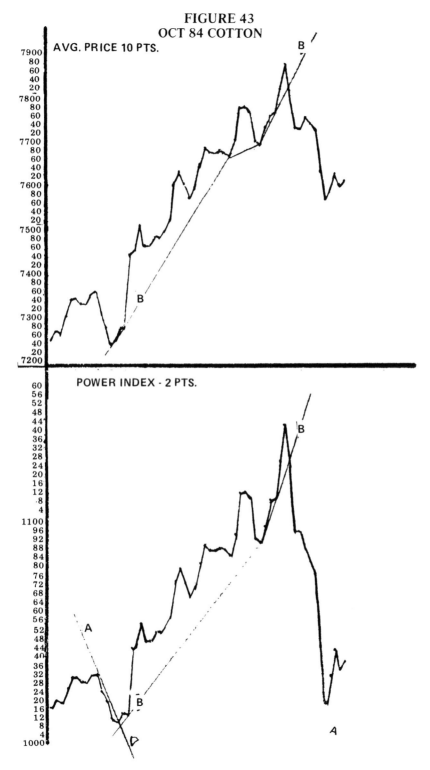

FIGURE 43
OCT 84 COTTON

139

FIGURE 44
OCT 84 COTTON

Start 1-26-84 To 4-19-84

HIGH	LOW	CLOSE	AVG.PR.	OPEN INT.	ADJ. OI
72.60	72.40	72.60	72.53	1,018	1018
72.86	72.60	72.86	72.77	1,035	1021
72.85	72.55	72.75	72.72	1,059	1020
73.35	72.79	73.20	73.11	1,065	1026
73.70	73.30	73.40	73.47	1,075	1031
73.60	73.40	73.50	73.50	1,107	1031
73.65	73.22	73.22	73.36	1,145	1029
73.45	73.15	73.45	73.35	1,171	1029
73.55	73.55	73.55	73.55	1,193	1032
73.70	73.50	73.50	73.57	1,207	1032
73.45	73.02	73.02	73.16	1,216	1025
73.15	72.75	72.75	72.88	1,252	1020
72.62	72.35	72.46	72.48	1,312	1013
72.90	72.25	72.65	72.60	1,309	1011
73.00	72.75	72.75	72.83	1,318	1015
72.80	72.80	72.80	72.80	1,321	1014
74.80	73.85	74.70	74.45	1,312	1044
74.85	74.10	74.80	74.58	1,289	1046
75.50	74.79	75.00	75.10	1,297	1055
74.90	74.45	74.55	74.63	1,306	1047
74.80	74.47	74.65	74.64	1,366	1047
75.25	74.50	74.85	74.87	1,371	1051
75.00	74.70	75.00	74.85	1,356	1051
75.00	74.90	75.00	74.97	1,353	1053
75.40	74.90	75.35	75.22	1,351	1058
76.25	75.65	76.15	76.02	1,384	1073
76.60	76.10	76.28	76.33	1,393	1079
76.15	75.95	75.99	76.03	1,454	1073
75.80	75.55	75.75	75.70	1,501	1066
76.20	75.70	76.00	75.97	1,519	1071
76.70	76.00	76.67	76.46	1,548	1081
77.00	76.65	76.85	76.83	1,615	1089
76.95	76.56	76.70	76.74	1,672	1087
76.85	76.60	76.75	76.73	1,732	1087
76.95	76.65	76.75	76.78	1,750	1088
76.85	76.55	76.75	76.72	1,763	1087
76.75	76.55	76.65	76.65	1,837	1085
77.25	76.65	77.15	77.02	1,895	1094
78.00	77.20	78.00	77.73	1,918	1112
78.00	77.60	77.65	77.75	1,986	1113
77.83	77.45	77.65	77.64	2,058	1110

FIGURE 44 (CONT'D)
OCT 84 COTTON

Start 1-26-84 To 4-19-84

HIGH	LOW	CLOSE	AVG.PR.	OPEN INT.	ADJ. OI
77.20	76.75	77.00	76.98	2,063	1092
77.12	76.60	76.95	76.89	2,064	1090
77.50	76.95	77.45	77.30	2,092	1101
77.80	77.45	77.50	77.58	2,124	1109
77.85	77.25	77.72	77.61	2,212	1110
78.40	77.80	78.30	78.17	2,255	1126
78.90	78.32	78.87	78.70	2,393	1142
78.30	77.90	78.15	78.12	2,567	1123
77.70	77.05	77.11	77.29	2,635	1095
77.40	77.05	77.40	77.28	2,764	1095
77.65	77.44	77.44	77.51	2,734	1087
77.55	77.15	77.40	77.37	2,704	1082
77.45	77.00	77.24	77.23	2,713	1077
76.95	75.80	76.15	76.30	2,692	1045
76.15	75.40	75.49	75.68	2,698	1023
76.10	75.59	76.05	75.91	2,754	1031
76.50	76.10	76.15	76.25	2,771	1043
76.15	75.90	75.96	76.00	2,814	1034
76.25	76.00	76.08	76.11	2,861	1038

141

Chapter 10

A Day-By-Day Trading History
—The Aug 85 Soybean Contract

For 89 days you and I will be walking through two trades, one long position and one short position. During the hypothetical trading, you will be privy to how I trade—with patience and discipline. Hopefully, you'll trade with discipline shortly, too.

Effective training requires interaction. Questions which may be on your mind will be answered as we plow through the four month period.

At the outset you may wonder why, of some 50 different contracts, I chose Soybeans. There are many reasons for that decision. Among them, commercials (bean processors and farmers) and speculators around the world trade Beans.

Trading is above reproach (hanky-panky) because news and information which might affect the price is instantly transmitted from one part of the globe to another part. Further, Soybeans are unique in that by-products (Meal and Oil) are also traded. The contract is highly liquid, which means a trade can be put on or offset with minimal price give-up (slippage).

Here are some questions you may have regarding this study:

Question: "How do you intend to compute profits and losses?"

Answer: "The PI signals develop after the market is closed. I will use the opening price on the next trading day to put on or offset a trade. In addition, a sixty dollar commission will be deducted from gross profits or added to any loss.''

Question: ''Seems fair enough. I noticed in reviewing the PI form that you did not include any trading data for April 5. What happened?''

Answer: ''From my recollection, there was no trading that day. I forget whether it was a bomb scare, computer problems or something.''

Question: ''Harold, I've got to laugh, why are you using the words, 'sitting and waiting'?''

Answer: ''I'll tell you. One of the greatest commodity traders of the 1920's was Jesse Livermore. He is reputed to have made millions trading commodities. He once said, 'I've made my money by sitting and waiting.' If I can get the readers of this book to sit and wait while in a trade or waiting for a trade, they may move out of the 90% bracket of losers into the 10% winner's circle.''

Question: ''Harold, as I checked over the first forty days, I noticed as the open interest was increasing, the adjusted open interest was decreasing. Can you explain this dichotomy?''

Answer: ''Yes, I can. The public trader looks at the open interest as a sign of price strength and weakness. As a matter of fact, trading rules based on the OI have been formulated. For example, if the OI is increasing as prices move higher, new buying is coming into the market, portending still higher prices. When the OI increases as prices fall, new shorts are putting on positions, in the expectation of still lower prices. Little, if anything, is said when prices trade within a four or five cent range.''

''The fly-in-the-ointment,'' in these rules and others regarding open interest is simply that they do not work. They are defective because most traders pay attention to the closing price, not the intra-day professional buying and selling strategies. How could they until now? The open interest, adjusted for professional trading activities as depicted, indicates a weakening price structure."

Question: "Are you suggesting, Harold, that your method of analysis measures the undercurrents of a market?"

Answer: "More than that, the Adjusted Open Interest figures, when graphed, show in bold relief the direction of prices for any contract studies."

Question: "Harold, on April 30th, the Average Price was $5.9917 with an Adjusted Open Interest of 1861. On Mar 8th, the Average Price was $5.9633 with an Adjusted Open Interest of 1883. A lower price with a higher open interest. Is there any significance between the price and Adjusted Open Interest on those dates?"

Answer: "Indeed, there is. Think for a moment, if there is a lower Adjusted Open Interest supporting a higher price, what do you think is going to happen? The Adjusted Open Interest is the foundation for support, not the raw daily open interest changes. They are meaningless."

"While I have not dealt with 'correlative analysis,' now may be a good time to discuss that subject. What it means as far as this work is concerned, is to compare Average Price and Adjusted Open Interest to different points of time with comparable Average Prices and Adjusted Open Interest figures. The analyst who checks these numbers may find added credence for remaining in a position. However, it is the graphed PI which will point the way to higher and lower prices, not correlative analysis."

"Keeping in mind that this type of analysis is not a trading guide, I'll give you the criteria involved. If, for example, today's Average Price has a lower Adjusted Open Interest at the same or close to a price of a few weeks ago, the underlying strength is ebbing and the probability of lower prices to come is high."

"When the Adjusted Open Interest is higher with an Average Price lower than it was in the past, look for a rally to commence shortly."

"Just remember, this form of analysis is not designed for trading purposes, nor can it be construed as an adjunct to the PI. The trading signals emanating from the PI graph are the only ones to trust."

At this time the raw data covering an 89 day period is finished and ready to graph. The time period begins Feb. 21, 1985 and concludes on June 27, 1985. The Power Index graphs and work forms (Figures 43 and 44) are on pages 150 through 153.

Day 1. Started the graphs. Sitting and waiting.

Day 2. Sitting and waiting.

Day 3. Sitting and waiting.

Day 4. A one day rally from Day 3. Sitting and waiting.

Day 5. Rally from Day 4 in PI continues. Sitting and waiting.

Day 6. PI rally is over. Second high established. Will draw a trendline from the high of Day 1 to the second lower PI high of Day 5. Point A.

Day 7. A slightly higher PI off the low of Day 6. Will extend trendline through the third high.

Day 8. Sitting and waiting.

Day 9. Trendline penetrated to upside on the PI. Tomorrow will go long one contract. The sitting and waiting for a PI signal is over.

Day 10. Went in at the opening of trading. The price I received is $5.92½. Now the sitting and waiting begins anew.

Day 11. Slight reaction in the PI. If it goes below the PI low on Day 8, I'll offset. If not, I'll just sit and wait.

Day 12. PI moving higher. The low PI on Day 8 looks as if it will hold.

Day 13. Another high on the PI. Good. Now I'll just sit and wait.

Day 14. A dip in the PI. Nothing to worry about.

Day 15. The dip was not violated from the previous day.

Day 16. Sitting and waiting.

Day 17. Sitting and waiting.

Day 18. Sitting and waiting.

Day 19. Sitting and waiting.

Day 20. Sitting and waiting.

Day 21. Sitting and waiting.

Day 22. Sitting and waiting.

Day 23. A day of caution. The PI low for the first time in almost two weeks took out a low. I'm now going to draw an upsloping trendline from Day 8 through Day 23. Point B.

Day 24. PI moved up right on the trendline.

Day 25. PI continues to follow trendline.

Day 26. PI trendline violated to the downside. Tomorrow will cancel the stop under the PI on Day 8 and offset Day 27. Closed out the long position and went short. Price received on the offset and new short position is $6.20.

To recap the first trade

Date In   Mar 6, '85 Long Position   Price $5.92½
Date Out Mar 29, '85 Offset - Short Price $6.20

Profit: 27½ Cts. = $1,375.00

| Commission: | $ 60.00 | Net Profit: $1,315.00 |
| Margin: | $500.00 | % Return on Equity: 263% |

Present position short one contract at $5.92½. Stop on PI above Day 26.

Day 28. Sitting and waiting.

Day 29. Sitting and waiting.

Day 30. Sitting and waiting.

Day 31. Sitting and waiting.

Day 32. Sitting and waiting.

Day 33. Sitting and waiting.

Day 34. Sitting and waiting.

Day 35. Sitting and waiting.

Day 36. PI violated the low of Day 34. Will now draw up-sloping trendline (from Day 29 just before the 6 day rally started in the PI connecting the low of Day 34, Point C).

147

Day 37. Sitting and waiting.
Day 38. Sitting and waiting.
Day 39. Sitting and waiting.
Day 40. Sitting and waiting.
Day 41. Sitting and waiting.
Day 42. Sitting and waiting.
Day 43. Sitting and waiting.
Day 44. Sitting and waiting.
Day 45. Sitting and waiting.
Day 46. Sitting and waiting.
Day 47. Sitting and waiting.
Day 48. Sitting and waiting.
Day 49. Sitting and waiting.
Day 50. Sitting and waiting.
Day 51. Sitting and waiting.
Day 52. Sitting and waiting.
Day 53. Sitting and waiting.
Day 54. Sitting and waiting.
Day 55. Sitting and waiting.
Day 56. Sitting and waiting.
Day 57. Sitting and waiting.
Day 58. Sitting and waiting.
Day 59. Sitting and waiting.
Day 60. Violation of the PI low on Day 54. Will draw trendline off the high of Day 45 to the high of Day 56. Point D.
Day 61. Sitting and waiting.
Day 63. Sitting and waiting
Day 64. Sitting and waiting.
Day 65. Sitting and waiting.
Day 66. Will extend trendline to high of yesterday.
Day 67. Sitting and waiting.
Day 68. Sitting and waiting.
Day 69. Sitting and waiting.
Day 70. Sitting and waiting.

Day 71. Will draw trendline through the high of day 70 to the bottom of the page.

Day 71. Sitting and waiting.

Day 72. Sitting and waiting.

Day 73. Trendline penetrated to the upside. Will offset short position tomorrow.

Day 74. Offset.

Recap—Second Trade. Short at $5.92½

Date In   Mar 29 '85

Date Out   Jun 6, '85   Price $5.6250

Profit: 30 Cts. = $1,500.00

Commission: $ 60.00   R Net Profit: $1,440.00

Margin: $500.00   % Return on Equity: 288%

In a 74 day period two positions were put on employing the PI. Total net profit came to $2,755.00, on a $500.00 margin. The total return in percentage terms is 551%!

While a long position could have been taken on Day 74, I think I've made my point. Trust the PI.

149

FIGURE 45
AUG 85 SOYBEANS

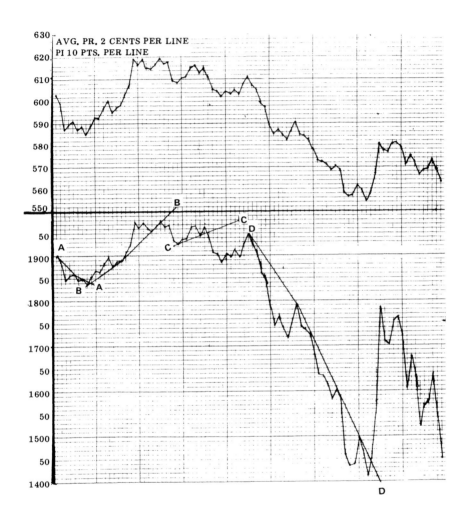

150

FIGURE 46
AUG 85 SOYBEANS

DATE	HIGH	LOW	CLOSE	AVG.PR.	OPEN INT.	ADJ. OI
2-21-85	605.50	597.50	605.25	602.75	1898	1898
22	601.50	597.50	598.50	599.17	1950	1886
25	590.00	584.00	588.75	587.58	1973	1848
26	593.00	587.00	589.50	589.83	1988	1856
27	595.00	588.00	589.50	590.83	2059	1859
28	589.00	586.50	587.25	587.58	2431	1846
3- 1-85	590.00	586.00	588.50	588.17	2527	1849
4	587.50	582.00	587.00	585.50	2377	1838
5	591.00	585.00	591.00	589.00	2470	1853
6	595.00	591.00	591.25	592.42	2459	1867
7	593.00	590.00	593.00	592.00	2471	1865
8	599.50	592.50	597.00	596.33	2484	1883
11	601.00	599.25	600.00	600.08	2457	1898
12	598.00	593.50	593.50	595.00	2454	1877
13	600.00	595.50	596.25	597.25	2417	1886
14	600.00	595.00	599.25	598.08	2410	1889
15	604.50	602.00	602.50	603.00	2397	1909
18	609.75	603.00	608.00	606.92	2420	1925
19	623.00	613.00	621.25	619.08	2426	1974
20	619.00	613.50	616.25	616.25	2433	1963
21	624.00	616.00	616.50	618.83	2279	1973
22	619.00	613.00	614.25	615.42	2386	1960
25	615.50	611.75	615.50	614.25	2612	1955
26	619.50	614.50	615.50	616.50	2596	1965
27	623.25	617.00	618.50	619.58	2616	1978
28	618.25	614.50	618.00	616.92	2781	1966
29	620.75	615.00	616.00	617.25	2872	1968
4- 1-85	612.50	608.50	608.50	609.83	2948	1933
2	610.00	606.00	610.00	608.67	2910	1927
3	612.50	608.50	609.50	610.17	2832	1934
4	612.50	607.50	612.00	610.67	3001	1936
8	618.25	611.00	618.00	615.75	3076	1962
9	619.75	614.50	614.75	616.33	3114	1965
10	617.00	610.50	610.75	612.75	3243	1946
11	617.00	613.50	616.50	615.67	3259	1962
12	618.50	608.00	608.00	611.50	3288	1940
15	610.50	603.00	603.75	605.75	3433	1908
16	607.00	601.50	605.25	604.58	3292	1902
17	606.75	598.75	600.50	602.00	3359	1888

151

FIGURE 46 (CONT'D)
AUG 85 SOYBEANS

DATE	HIGH	LOW	CLOSE	AVG.PR.	OPEN INT.	ADJ. OI
4-18-85	605.50	602.00	604.75	604.08	3988	1902
19	605.50	600.00	605.00	603.50	4083	1898
22	608.00	603.50	605.00	605.50	4188	1912
23	605.25	601.25	604.00	603.50	4115	1898
24	610.00	604.00	610.00	608.00	4079	1928
25	615.00	609.50	609.50	611.33	3900	1949
26	609.50	606.50	606.50	607.50	4072	1923
29	609.00	603.50	604.00	605.50	4462	1908
30	604.75	595.50	597.25	599.17	4530	1861
5- 1-85	599.50	594.50	597.25	597.08	4596	1845
2	596.00	586.25	587.50	589.92	4862	1787
3	589.50	583.00	583.00	585.17	5061	1746
6	589.75	582.50	589.25	587.17	5077	1763
7	592.50	579.00	582.00	584.50	4966	1740
8	584.50	579.50	582.50	582.17	5158	1719
9	589.00	583.50	587.25	586.58	5273	1759
10	591.50	588.00	591.25	590.25	5104	1791
13	589.00	581.25	583.75	584.67	5031	1743
14	586.75	581.75	584.25	584.25	5015	1739
15	586.25	580.25	581.50	582.67	5269	1725
16	582.50	575.00	576.50	578.00	5638	1680
17	577.50	571.25	572.75	573.83	5768	1638
20	575.25	570.25	574.75	573.42	5756	1634
21	576.50	568.50	569.00	571.33	5837	1613
22	570.75	565.00	570.00	568.58	6567	1581
23	571.75	568.25	571.00	570.33	6648	1601
24	571.25	566.50	568.00	568.58	6652	1581
28	565.00	555.00	555.25	558.42	6790	1460
29	558.25	555.25	556.00	556.50	6559	1437
30	558.00	554.00	558.00	556.67	6381	1439
31	565.00	559.00	561.75	561.92	6276	1498
6- 3-85	563.75	557.00	557.25	559.33	6264	1469
4	556.00	552.50	554.50	554.33	6250	1413
5	561.50	554.75	560.25	558.83	6671	1467
6	570.00	562.50	569.50	567.33	7342	1579
7	590.00	571.00	587.00	582.67	7604	1785
10	580.00	574.25	577.75	577.33	8148	1710
11	580.50	569.50	580.25	576.75	8277	1702
12	586.75	577.00	577.25	580.33	8592	1755
13	583.50	575.50	583.25	580.75	8475	1761

FIGURE 46 (CONT'D)
AUG 85 SOYBEANS

DATE	HIGH	LOW	CLOSE	AVG.PR.	OPEN INT.	ADJ. OI
6-14-85	585.00	574.00	575.25	578.08	8,554	1722
17	572.50	568.50	572.00	571.00	9,305	1608
18	577.00	571.50	576.25	574.92	9,978	1676
19	575.75	570.25	571.25	572.42	10,185	1632
20	569.00	564.50	566.25	566.58	10,404	1526
21	572.25	565.00	569.50	568.92	10,063	1568
24	571.50	566.00	571.25	569.58	9,281	1579
25	576.00	571.25	571.75	573.00	9,632	1637
26	572.50	566.00	566.25	568.25	10,576	1549
27	566.00	562.00	562.25	563.42	11,594	1450

Chapter 11

Option Trading
Using The Power Index

My research has shown that by using options tactics based on long and short Power Index signals off the futures contracts, you can, in many cases, maximize your potential for profit. You can increase the risk/reward ratio, thereby lowering the risk to the cost of the option while allowing for unlimited profit appreciation during the life of the option.

I dare say that thousands upon thousands of would-be speculators have stayed out of the futures markets because they do not have the substantial capital needed to open a commodity trading account with most brokerage firms. Also, these same speculators do not possess the emotional make-up of futures traders in general. One should not deduce that option trading is the purview of small traders. More and more, as additional futures contracts become optionable, virtually all segments of traders, large and small, commercial and public are turning to the options markets.

You always know your total risk in options trading—if you are an options buyer.

YOU ALWAYS KNOW YOUR
TOTAL RISK IN OPTIONS TRADING—
IF YOU ARE AN OPTIONS BUYER

The only risk an options buyer assumes is the cost of the option. Yet, as I mentioned, there is no limit to the profit return to the option holder.

WHAT IS AN OPTION?

An option is an instrument which gives the owner (holder, purchaser) the right but not the obligation to (a) buy or sell a futures contract at (b) a specified price and (c) within a specified period of time.

OPTION LIQUIDITY

An option can be bought or sold (transferred) as easily as a futures contract on the respective exchange. You simply call your broker to buy or sell an option and, within a matter of minutes, the order is executed.

WHAT IS A CALL OPTION?

A call option (or simply, "a call") is the right but not the obligation to buy a futures contract at a specified price within a specified period of time.

WHAT IS A PUT OPTION?

A put option (or simply, "a put") gives the purchaser the right but not the obligation to sell a futures contract at a specified price within a specified period of time.

PROFITING ON A PURCHASE
OF A CALL OPTION

A call is bought in anticipation of an appreciation in the price of the futures contract prior to the expiration of the call. In simple terms, suppose you purchase a call on the Nov. Soybean contract with a 'strike' price of $5.25. As the futures price moves and possibly surpasses $5.25, the call will increase in value.

PROFITING ON THE PURCHASE
OF A PUT OPTION

A put is purchased in anticipation of the price of the futures contract moving lower. Assume you purchase a $5.25 put on the Nov. Soybean contract. As the futures contract's price moves further and further below the strike price of the put, its value will increase.

USING THE POWER INDEX
TO TRADE OPTIONS

The few rules are easy to follow. When a long or short signal is triggered on the optionable futures contract, buy the call or put option whose strike price is closest to the price of the futures contract. When a reversal Power Index signal is generated, offset (sell) the option and reverse your position.

DICTIONARY OF OPTION TERMINOLOGY

Strike Price: The price of the option. Each option has one expiration month and one strike price. At present, Soybean put and call options are traded in multiples of twenty-five cents, above and below the price of the futures contract. For example, the Nov. 1985 Soybean contract has the following call and put strike prices.

Calls	Puts
$4.75	$4.75
5.00	5.00
5.25	5.25
5.50	5.50
5.75	5.75
6.00	6.00

The closing price for Nov. Soybeans on Sep. 24, 1985 is $5.22. If there was a Power Index signal suggesting higher prices, then you would purchase the $5.25 call, since that is closest to the present value of the Nov. contract. Conversely, had the Power Index flashed a sell signal, you would purchase the $5.25 put option. The call option at $5.25 is called an out-of-the-money option, because its strike price is above the futures price. The put option at $5.25 is an in-the-money option because the price of the futures contract is below the options strike price. Thus, since the put gains in value as the futures price moves lower, its premium would be higher than the same strike price on the call. And it is. On this date the premium on the $5.25 Nov. call is 7¾ cents while that of the put is 10-1/8 cents.

A one cent move in the grain complex is equal to fifty ($50.00) dollars. A 1/8 cent move is equal to $6.25. There is a minor difference in fluctuations between a grain contract and its option. Grain contract prices move in ¼ cent ($12.50) increments, while grain options move in 1/8 cent increments.

Exercise Price: The price of the option at which it can be exercised (tendered) for the particular commodity.

Options Writer: One who writes the option. The writer receives the premium (see below) for the option. This premium varies depending on the present price of the contract, time left to expiration of the option, etc.

At-The-Money: An option whose strike price is the same as the futures price.

In-The-Money: An option (call or put) whose strike price is above or below the present price of the contract. In the case of a call, it is said to be in-the-money when its strike price is below the price of the contract. A put is in-the-money when its strike price is above that of the contract.

Out-of-The Money: A call whose strike price is above the futures contract price. A put whose strike price is below the contract's price.

Option Buyer: The purchaser of an option.

Option Premium: The price paid for an option.

Expiration Date: The date an option expires.

Option Month: The month in which the option expires (see expiration date). Options are traded in the same months as the contract.

Time Value: A component whose value is included in the premium. The longer the life of the option, the higher is the premium.

Conclusion

Throughout this book, one inescapable fact emerges: man is governed by and is a slave to his emotions. Therefore, predictable responses to stimuli are measurable. The result as it applies to futures trading is predictable, too! Profits should accrue to those who are capable of controlling their own emotions while acting on those of others based on the Power Index.

It is my conviction that a key to profitable speculation is specialization. You cannot expect success if you trade spreads one week, options the next week, then net positions. To be a master of one trading medium is preferable to being an apprentice in numerous trading mediums.

I have given you the tools—take them and use them. You will not be sorry.

Good luck and profitable trading.

Harold Goldberg